SURVIVING & THRIVING

WITH TEACHER ACTION RESEARCH

Critical Pedagogical Perspectives

Greg S. Goodman, *General Editor*

Vol. 33

The Educational Psychology series is part of the Peter Lang Education list.
Every volume is peer reviewed and meets
the highest quality standards for content and production.

PETER LANG
New York • Bern • Frankfurt • Berlin
Brussels • Vienna • Oxford • Warsaw

SURVIVING & THRIVING WITH TEACHER ACTION RESEARCH

Reflections and Advice from the Field

EDITED BY HEATHER LATTIMER & STACEY CAILLIER

PETER LANG
New York • Bern • Frankfurt • Berlin
Brussels • Vienna • Oxford • Warsaw

Library of Congress Cataloging-in-Publication Data

Surviving and thriving with teacher action research: reflections
and advice from the field / edited by Heather Lattimer, Stacey Caillier.
pages cm — (Educational psychology: critical pedagogical perspectives; vol. 33)
Includes bibliographical references.
1. Action research in education. 2. Teaching—United States. I. Lattimer, Heather.
LB1028.24.S895 370.72—dc23 2015003547
ISBN 978-1-4331-2988-9 (hardcover)
ISBN 978-1-4331-2987-2 (paperback)
ISBN 978-1-4539-1526-4 (e-book)
ISSN 1943-8109

Bibliographic information published by **Die Deutsche Nationalbibliothek.**
Die Deutsche Nationalbibliothek lists this publication in the "Deutsche
Nationalbibliografie"; detailed bibliographic data are available
on the Internet at http://dnb.d-nb.de/.

Cover design by Marius Ty Jefferson

The paper in this book meets the guidelines for permanence and durability
of the Committee on Production Guidelines for Book Longevity
of the Council of Library Resources.

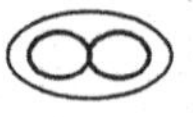

Printed in the United States of America

Table of Contents

Acknowledgments

The strength of this book is in the voices of teacher researchers who share their stories. Many, many thanks to each of our authors for your willingness to take a risk and share both the joys and the challenges of engaging in this work in classrooms alongside students. Your contributions exemplify the dedication and generosity of so many K–16 educators—thank you!

Many thanks also to our students and professional colleagues who have pushed our thinking and encouraged our work in action research over the years. We have learned and continue to learn best when immersed in the work alongside thoughtful, engaged individuals who ask important questions and offer unique perspectives.

Thank you to the editors at Peter Lang. We greatly appreciate your support, professionalism, and commitment to excellence throughout the publishing process.

Thank you to Marius (Ty) Jefferson, a senior at High Tech High Media Arts, who created a beautiful design for the cover.

Finally, thank you to our families and friends for your understanding and encouragement. Your support allows us to pursue work that matters.

Introduction

STACEY CAILLIER AND HEATHER LATTIMER

What do you think of when you think of research? What are your experiences with research?

When faced with these questions, many of us conjure up images of science labs with hypotheses to test, stacks of books and printed articles to read, and lonely hours hunched over a computer. Those of us with a humanities or social science background might describe research as a process of collecting and summarizing the ideas of others in order to build support for an argument or a recommendation. Those of us with a background in the physical sciences might describe a process of forming hypotheses, testing those hypotheses, and describing what is found in "objective" terms that require the researcher to remove him/herself from the equation. We might describe research as a process that concludes when the data or evidence has been collected and analyzed, the conclusions stated, and the implications and next steps reported. Researchers' responsibilities seemingly end here; it is the responsibility of others to implement researchers' recommendations. In short, it is the work of practitioners, those who work in the contexts being studied, to take action and to effect change.

It is not surprising, then, that for many of us educators, the concept of "action research" can at first seem like an oxymoron. Our experience has been that teachers often express excitement and relief upon learning what action research is—that it engages educators as researchers and scholars, that it is rooted in their daily wonderings and practical concerns about teaching and learning, and that it can be a powerful tool for transforming schools and schooling.

In contrast to more traditional forms of research that tend to emphasize the development of theory over practical application, action research is a systematic inquiry conducted for the purpose of not just understanding, but improving, organizations and their practices. Moreover, action research is designed and conducted by "insiders" who analyze the data to improve their own practice and the systems in which they work. Teacher action research—which usually involves ongoing cycles of inquiry, action, and reflection—has been described as "a natural extension of good teaching" (Hubbard & Power, 1999, p. 3), a tool for improving schooling for students and their families (Noffke & Stevenson, 1995), a venue for professionalizing teaching by promoting a teacher-generated knowledge base (Grossman, 2003), and a vehicle for critiquing, challenging, and ultimately altering elements of schooling that perpetuate inequities (Kincheloe, 1991).

While teacher action research has been around for decades, it has gained momentum in recent years as educational reforms have increasingly taken the form of external mandates, positioning teachers as implementers rather than designers of change efforts and curricula. In their review of teacher research since the 1980s, Cochran-Smith and Lytle note, "the intellectual and educational projects that fueled the current U.S. teacher researcher movement had in common a critique—either implicit or explicit—of prevailing concepts of the teacher as technician, consumer, receiver, transmitter, and implementer of other people's knowledge" (1999, p. 16). The experts and policymakers who develop and mandate reforms are not the only ones implicated in this critique; the emergence of teacher research also served as a challenge to the authority of universities as the exclusive gatekeepers and contributors to the knowledge base of teaching. The sentiments expressed by Berthoff (1987) and quoted here by Cochran-Smith and Lytle parallel those we hear often from teachers: "[T]eachers do not need more findings from university-based researchers, but more dialogue with other teachers that would generate theories grounded in practice" (1999, p. 15).

In this way, action research can be a tool for liberation. It challenges the distinctions between theory and practice, between knower and doer. The practice of teaching is inherently laden with theory, and useful theory develops from practice. Teacher researchers, as insiders, are in a unique and powerful position, not only to contribute to the knowledge base of teaching and learning, but also to use that knowledge to effect change within their classrooms, schools, and communities. The questions for all of us engaged in action research are then: How do we support each other in generating understandings and actions that will lead to improved practice and the positive transformation of schools? And equally important, how do we learn from each other along the way?

This book is an attempt to answer these questions.

Anyone who has experienced action research knows it can be exhilarating and exhausting. The process of action research is professional, political, and deeply personal. It pushes us to reconsider our beliefs and helps us arrive at new revelations. It requires us to have faith in the process and to persevere through frustration and self-doubt. It inspires us to see our students and our colleagues through new eyes, and to recommit to the hard but deeply meaningful work of teaching and learning. From developing questions, to crafting research designs, to making sense of our data, to finding our voice so that we can share our learning, action research continually pushes us to become more thoughtful about our practice and more engaged in the professional dialogue about education.

There are many books on the market that outline the mechanics of action research. There are a few excellent books that describe the iterative and evolving process of action research. What is often missing, however, are the voices of those engaged in action research, those who can speak to the *lived experience* of doing action research in schools.

This book is about those experiences. It is for teacher action researchers, by teacher action researchers.

In the chapters that follow, action researchers share moments of insight, offer encouragement and advice, and reflect on lessons learned about the action research process. Each chapter was written with the busy teacher in mind, to be read in 15 minutes during your lunch hour or before or after school. Each of the sections in this volume—which discuss issues from the journey toward a research question, to trusting the process, to sharing and embodying action research—includes a brief introduction that suggests questions to reflect on as you read. We hope that these questions, like action research, support you in exploring multiple perspectives, reflecting on your own practice, and generating new questions and actions of your own.

Whether you are engaged in collaborative action research or pursuing action research independently, we hope that this text becomes a friend and confidant—guiding and inspiring you throughout the wonderful, wonderfully challenging, and ultimately transformative work of conducting action research in schools.

WORKS CITED

Berthoff, A. (1987). The teacher as RE-searcher. In D. Gosmani & P. Stillman (eds.), *Reclaiming the classroom: Teacher research as an agency for change* (pp. 28–38). Upper Montclair, NJ: Boynton/Cook.

Cochran-Smith, M., & Lytle, S. (1999). The teacher research movement: A decade later. *Educational Researcher*, 28(7), 15–25.

Grossman, P. (2003, January/February). Teaching: From a nation at risk to a profession at risk? *Harvard Education Letter*. Retrieved February 26, 2008, from http:www.edletter.org/past/issues/2003-jf/nation.shtml.

Hubbard, R., & Power, B. (1999). *Living the questions: A guide for teacher-researchers*. York, ME: Stenhouse Publishers.

Kincheloe, J. (1991). *Teachers as researchers: Qualitative inquiry as a path to empowerment*. London: The Falmer Press.

Noffke, S., & Stevenson, R. (1995). *Educational action research: Becoming practically critical*. New York, NY: Teachers College Press.

SECTION ONE

Journey TOWARD A Research Question

Action research begins when we notice challenges, opportunities, and interactions in our classrooms and begin to ask questions. "Why did this lesson work so much better in 1st period than in 3rd?" "How can I reach my students who struggle with math?" "Will this assessment really show what my students have learned?" "How can I make this curriculum more engaging?" These questions, informal wonderings that constantly swirl in teachers' minds, can be the starting point for an AR journey. As Ruth Shagoury and Brenda Power write in their book on teacher research, *Living the Questions*, "We don't always start out with a specific, clearly formulated question. As observers of classrooms daily, we can unearth our questions by reflecting on what we see" (2012, p. 20)

Action research may originate from something that surprises us; those moments or interactions that seem out of place to our usual routine can spur questions that lead to larger investigations. It can derive from an area of concern; frustrations over what appears to not be working can be ripe for further inquiry. It can come from the tensions that often exist between expectations and reality—our own expectations, administrators' expectations, policy demands, and curriculum promises often collide with what we observe in our classrooms; these tensions are ripe for research.

And, contrary to common belief that action research has to address a "problem," research questions can also be born out of areas of strength and success. In their book on individual and institutional change, Chip and Dan Heath argue that meaningful change often stems from recognizing unexpected successes, what they term "bright spots." They write, "[T]o pursue bright spots is to ask the question 'what's working and how can we do more of it?' Sounds simple, doesn't it? Yet, in the real world, this obvious questions is almost never asked" (2010, p. 45). Recognizing successes in our classrooms and creating action research questions in response to those successes can help us leverage that success to improve our teaching and strengthen student learning.

Once you've identified a problem, concern, tension, or success that is ripe for further study, it is worth sitting with it for awhile, peering at it from different angles, and doing some initial investigation before officially adopting a research question. Many action researchers find it useful to assess needs in their classroom by making more structured observations or looking more closely at student work, to talk with students, even younger children, to get their interpretations and better understand their experiences in the classroom, and to share nascent ideas with colleagues to gather additional suggestions and to clarify their thinking. These early explorations can significantly strengthen the quality of the question and the research. Teacher and researcher JoAnn Portalupi cautions, "Don't rush to form a question so your research can begin. Figuring out the question is an important part of the research. Once you've arrived you will look back and see that you are already deeply involved in the work of conducting a classroom-based inquiry, one that will guide the learning of both you and your students" (2012, p. 33).

Although there is no formula for arriving at a question to guide your action research, there are a few criteria that generally characterize good research questions. In my own work with graduate students, we often speak of the three "Ms"—meaningful, measurable, and manageable. It is essential that the question you arrive at is meaningful—you will be spending time investigating this question in your classroom, and it will shape your classroom practice, influence your interactions with students, and be present in your conversations with colleagues. It needs to be what author Ralph Fletcher (1996) calls a "fierce wondering," a question that grips you and won't let you go. It should be focused around something that you care about and designed to guide an investigation that you believe will improve the quality of the teaching and learning experience in your classroom.

The question also needs to be measurable. You want to be able to learn something through your investigation and, hopefully, to share that learning with others. To do so, you'll need to collect data through observations, assessments, student feedback, interviews, and video analysis. Anticipating the types of data you'll want to collect, what Donald Graves (1994) termed "tunneling," can help to refine and focus the research question. It is important, however, that the question not become too focused. Avoid yes/no questions; these leave little room for exploration and prevent us from capturing the nuances and unexpected discoveries that are an essential part of action research. And avoid setting up an experimental design; action research is not the place to test a claim on children by establishing a control group and an experimental group. Classrooms are much too complex to reduce teaching and learning to an either/or duality.

Finally, the question needs to be manageable. If you are undertaking action research, it likely means that you already have a full-time job as a practitioner, or perhaps you are sharing classroom responsibilities as a student teacher or intern. Recognizing the limitations pressed upon us by time and context is essential if we are to be successful in action research. If this is your first time out (or even if you've been doing action research for years), you are unlikely to solve all of the problems in the universe through action research. Be reasonable. Choose a focused question that you can really explore from multiple angles in the time and space available to you. We are often surprised that by pulling on one seemingly small thread through AR, the fabric of the classroom reveals itself in a new way and multiple aspects of teaching and learning can be transformed.

The chapters in this first section of the book explore how seven teacher researchers journeyed to create research questions that were meaningful, measurable, and manageable.

In the first chapter, Callie Sprague describes the sometimes messy process of identifying a research topic. As is the case for many novice teacher researchers, Callie initially felt overwhelmed by the research possibilities. She had so many questions and wonderings, but at first nothing resonated as a researchable topic. In her chapter she describes her own process of moving from many musings to a focused research topic, and offers practical tips for other teacher researchers for strategies that can be used to identify potential topics in their own classrooms.

The next three chapters offer examples of three different entry points into research. First, in chapter 2, Linnea Rademaker, Catherine Henry, and Laurel Gustafson describe how their research started in response to concerns about students who didn't seem to be responding to the literacy curriculum in their school. Sharing their frustrations while floating in the pool on a lazy summer day prompted a recognition that more systematic investigation was needed, and an action research project was born. Margit Boyesen initiated her research due to a healthy skepticism about the potential impact of implementing the district's technology plan. In her chapter, she describes her concerns about the disruptions that adopting iPads in the classroom might bring, and her decision to create an action research project to investigate. Her research was born out of the dilemma resulting from a district requirement that didn't feel like it consistently fit with her instructional philosophy—a recognition that learning with technology is part of the 21st century but a concern that too much screen time might diminish classroom community. In the fourth chapter, JoHanna Simko describes how her research started from a desire to explore the potential benefits of transplanting a past classroom success into a new school context. She'd observed great benefits in engaging students in a peer mentoring structure in her previous school, and wanted to see if a similar program could reap similar rewards in her new school. Her AR aimed to focus on a "bright spot." Three very different avenues into action research—one starting from a concern about student performance, another in response to a dilemma about a district reform, and the third working to transplant an earlier success into a new context—demonstrate the range of ideas that can give rise to action research investigations.

The next two chapters address the challenge of crafting action research questions. First, Qudsia Kalsoom recounts her struggle to find the "perfect" question. Just as action research differs in approach and methodology from more traditional forms of qualitative and quantitative research, so, too, action research questions differ from traditional research questions. AR isn't setting out to "prove" something; instead, we are setting out to "learn," and the questions we ask must allow room for learning to take place. Qudsia's chapter provides a strong example of the evolution of a research question as it turns into an action research question, and offers practical tips about pitfalls to avoid and strategies for success as you frame out your own AR question. Jocelyn Peck's chapter also addresses the challenge of crafting a research question. She focuses on the importance of identifying research questions that grapple with the root causes of concerns in the classroom rather than simply responding to what might be readily visible symptoms. She shares how she used previously collected data, conversations with students, and intentionally designed needs assessment tools to uncover the sources of the frustration her math students displayed and to identify potential solutions that would become the focus of her research. Jocelyn acknowledges that this process led her to an unexpected and initially somewhat disconcerting research question, and challenges readers to be open to new possibilities when crafting their questions.

Finally, Ashley Vasquez shares an account of her anxiety in getting the research process started, from sorting through early ideas to forming a research question to getting started in the classroom. Her story resonates with the experience of many novice teacher researchers who may at times struggle to limit the scope of the work. Her realization that this research study is just one project and didn't need to, in her words, "end world hunger" helps us all remember that our work as educators is a career-long process of continual growth and improvement. One action research project needn't set out to solve every challenge in the classroom ... though it is often amazing that by pulling on one strand of the web of classroom practice and looking closely at teaching and learning in our classrooms through AR, many new ideas, learnings, and transformations are uncovered.

As you read the accounts presented here, here are a few questions to consider as you think about your own teaching and research:

- What prompted each of these authors to pursue research in their classrooms?

- What are the challenges, concerns, tensions, or successes in your classroom? What are your "fierce wonderings"?
- How did these authors frame their action research questions? How did they keep their questions meaningful, measurable, and manageable? How did they avoid the pitfall of trying to "prove" something with their research, and create open-ended AR questions that left space for new discovery?
- How might you frame AR questions that respond to areas of research interest in your own classroom?

WORKS CITED

Fletcher, R. (1996). *A writer's notebook: Unlocking the writer within you.* New York: HarperCollins.

Graves, D. (1994). *A fresh look at writing.* Portsmouth, NH: Heinemann.

Heath, C., & Heath, D. (2010). *Switch: How to change things when change is hard.* New York: Crown.

Portalupi, J. (2012). Strategies for working toward a research question. In R. Shagoury & B. M. Power, *Living the questions: A guide for teacher-researchers* (2nd ed.) (pp. 30–32). Portland, ME: Stenhouse.

Shagoury, R., & Power, B. M. (2012). *Living the questions: A guide for teacher-researchers* (2nd ed.). Portland, ME: Stenhouse.

CHAPTER ONE

Fierce Wonderings

Finding Your Research Passion

CALLIE SPRAGUE

> I like the challenge of being with the 5th graders in our combo class but I wish we could do the science project like the other 4th graders. I miss having more friends from my own grade in my class. Sometimes it's good to be different but sometimes I wish we could just be with everyone else our age.
>
> —SARAH, GRADE 4

The beginning of my action research process was also the beginning of a new student teaching placement. Enrolled in a combined master's and credential program, my cohort colleagues and I began to take on our role as action researchers at about the same time that we were transitioning into a second semester of student teaching. For me, this placement was in a 4th/5th combination class. Everything was new—new school, new classroom, new grade level, new role.

When our AR instructor asked us to record our observations and begin to ask questions in the form of "fierce wonderings"—musings about our classrooms and pedagogy more generally—a list seemed easy to generate. I wondered how the strong focus on technology was impacting student learning and how I could maximize its effectiveness. I wondered how to help Vitor, a new student who had just moved from Brazil, develop his English language skills and adapt socially. I wondered about project-based learning, a pedagogical approach that provoked a personal interest. I wondered how I could support Kate, a 5th grader with a learning disability and really low self-esteem, to feel more confident and motivated. I wondered how I was going to challenge Abby and Michael, 5th graders who mastered concepts quickly and were always driven to do more. I wondered how to help a group of 4th grade boys who were constantly getting into trouble for bullying other students.

I had an abundance of wonderings, but none of them felt "fierce." I was looking for the technically perfect AR question—one that would be meaningful, measurable, and manageable. I had been approaching my wonderings from a technical perspective. I felt like I was supposed to wonder about EL students, technology in the classroom, and pedagogy, and I did wonder about these things, but these wonderings weren't the ones that kept me up at night.

In an email to my AR advisor around this time, I wrote, "I know that we are supposed to be 'getting engaged' with our questions, but I'm having serious cold feet." I was putting a lot of pressure on myself to formulate the perfect question and in turn, I was having a lot of trouble committing to one. I had been looking forward to doing AR. It was a chance to help my students, a chance to learn how to be a better teacher, and after completing the heavily structured state credentialing assessment, it was a chance to try something that *I* was curious about. That choice was exhilarating, but for a person who takes an hour to choose what kind of sandwich to order for lunch, committing to an AR question wasn't easy.

I knew that I would have to live with this question for several months and that I would spend a significant amount of time thinking, planning, collecting data, and writing about the question that I chose. I didn't feel passionate enough about any of these questions to commit that amount of time and work to researching them. I wanted a question that didn't have an easy technical answer. I wanted a question that was worthy of research. I wanted a question that would truly make a difference for all of my students.

As I tried to navigate my wonderings and find the perfect AR topic, it suddenly dawned on me that I had been missing something big. "I like the challenge of being with the 5th graders in our combo class but I wish we could do the science project like the other 4th graders." I was brought back to a conversation with my 4th grader about being in a combination class. "Sometimes it's good to be different but sometimes I wish we could just be with everyone else our age."

The 4th/5th grade combo design was something so intertwined with this classroom that I didn't originally see it as a potential action research topic. But the challenges and opportunities that come with a multigrade classroom were the concerns that kept me awake at night. They occupied my thoughts as I planned and taught lessons, they were the source of many long phone calls to my mom, and they were questions that I couldn't find answers to in a book. The construct of a multigrade classroom itself was my "fierce wondering."

In truth, I had wondered about the structure, purpose, and efficiency of combination classrooms since I first arrived several weeks earlier. Growing up in small town in Massachusetts, I had never seen nor even heard of a combination classroom before, and the concept initially seemed somewhat overwhelming. My cooperating teacher planned and instructed two separate math, science, and social studies lessons every day. She had one grade level doing independent work while she gave instruction to the other, and then they would switch. She orchestrated this skillfully, but I knew that planning and teaching for two grade levels was an immense challenge, and I worried that I might not be able to manage when it was my turn to take over the class.

However, as I began to consider the multigrade classroom through a teacher researcher lens, my focus shifted from the difficulties it posed for me as a teacher to the opportunities and challenges that a 4th/5th combo class raised for my students. I wanted to know what students could learn from each other, how we could capitalize on the strengths of having a multiage classroom, and how we could make our classroom feel more united. The more I observed in the classroom, listened to students, talked with my advisor, and shared with my cohort-mates, the more passionate I became about this topic. I had found the "fierce wondering" that would guide my research focus.

As you navigate your own wonderings and work to identify an AR question that is meaningful to you, below are some practical tips that may help.

ASK YOURSELF: WHAT IS UNIQUE ABOUT MY CLASSROOM?

As I was listing my wonderings early on in the process, I found myself listing the topics that I had heard before, the ones that I knew were acceptable AR topics, the ones that were usually the names of courses I had taken—Supporting Students with Intellectual Disabilities in the General Ed Classroom, Technology and Instruction, and Teaching ESL Students. However, when I stepped away from these topics and really looked at my classroom and my students, I found much more depth. Every classroom is unique, and action research is meant to address a topic that is specific to your classroom and your students. Take the time to notice what is unique about your classroom: What are the strengths? What are the challenges? What are your students interested in? How do your students interact with each other? What opportunities do you see in your classroom or at your school? This will help you narrow your search for a question, and will, I hope, help you find a question that is organic and true to your students.

LISTEN TO YOUR STUDENTS

Your classroom observations are incredibly valuable, but your students have a perspective that you don't have. They see the things in the classroom that you miss, they interact with each other outside of the classroom, and they see and hear things that you, as their teacher, are simply not included in. They experience the same classroom in a completely different way than you do, and they are perceptive to the strengths and challenges that it has. When I listened to my 4th grader explain that she felt like she was missing out on what other 4th graders were doing, but she also thought she was learning more than she would in a straight 4th grade class, my understanding of the classroom shifted. It wasn't just about making sure that each grade level got the content that they were supposed to get; it was about making sure that each student felt like part of a community within our classroom. Ask your students what they think about their classroom and listen to what they have to say.

CHOOSE A QUESTION THAT YOU ARE ACTUALLY WONDERING ABOUT

You are probably already wondering about many aspects of your teaching. As teachers, we have dedicated ourselves to our students, but teaching is complicated, and you probably have questions about why we do what we do and how to do it better. You might be wondering about a particular student, or a group of students, or your whole class, or maybe you are wondering about schoolwide practices, or maybe you're wondering about yourself as a teacher. We certainly don't have all of the answers, so what is it that you want to know? AR is an opportunity for you to learn more about something that you really want to know more about, so take advantage of it by answering a question that you truly have. On top of that, choose a question that doesn't have a clear answer or a technical solution. I got caught up in wonderings that were mechanical and technical; they were passing curiosities, but they weren't truly puzzling. Choose something that warrants research and deserves your time. Use this opportunity not only to help your students, but to help you grow as an educator.

Looking back at my experience with action research, I feel satisfied with the work that I did in my classroom and with the learning that I took away from my research. Because I chose a topic that was grounded in the specific context of my classroom, I was able to sustain my own interest through the process, provide a meaningful experience for my students, and truly make a difference in my classroom. Beyond the changes that I made in that classroom, I learned to approach each of my future classes with a researcher lens. Every class has its own unique set of strengths and challenges, and as teachers, we need to recognize them and take time to learn what works for each group of students. Though choosing an action research topic may feel overwhelming, don't feel confined by finding the technically perfect topic. Be true to your students and to your own fierce wonderings. Ask the question that you really want the answer to, and enjoy the process of finding it.

CHAPTER TWO

Starting WITH A Problem

Using Action Research to Respond to Challenges in the Classroom

LINNEA RADEMAKER, CATHERINE HENRY, AND LAUREL GUSTAFSON

INTRODUCTION

Cathy: One hot, summer afternoon I floated in my backyard pool, talking with a friend, as I often did, about schools and schooling. My friend, Linnea, is a professor who teaches education and action research courses at a local university. On this particular afternoon we were talking about several children with whom I work at a nearby elementary school. I'm a special education teacher working with students in 1st and 2nd grade who need extra services—both in the classroom (with Laurel, a 2nd grade teacher, whom you will meet below) and outside the classroom in "pull out" time. School would be starting again in a few weeks, and I was busy planning for the first week of school. These children that we spoke of were in 2nd grade, and each had special education Individualized Education Plans (IEPs), with documented disabilities in a variety of physical, behavioral, and academic areas. Each student required support services for assistance in reaching his or her academic potential. I expressed frustration that after working with these students in 1st grade, I had not been able to help them progress more in their literacy-skills development. I described a literacy program that the school had purchased but was not currently using. The school required the use of the assessments from the program as part of the regular literacy curriculum, but at that time it did not require the use of the program itself in daily classroom lessons. I had reviewed the program and wondered if it would be an alternative way to help these same children, now in 2nd grade, each of whom was still struggling in literacy development. I thought that this program might provide a differentiated starting point for children who had trouble grasping various concepts related to phonics and literacy. At that point Linnea tentatively offered, "I could help you set up an action research project to see if it worked, if you want."

DIVERSE PERCEPTIONS OF OUR "TENTATIVE" BEGINNING

Linnea: Tentatively was the way I approached this idea, because when I first suggested this project to Cathy, I wasn't sure that she would be very excited about the idea, as I knew the demands Cathy faced as a special education teacher. I also knew from working with preservice teachers that many were skeptical about their ability to continue to practice action research in their new classrooms upon graduating from their teacher training programs. I was afraid of pushing Cathy too hard. I believed strongly that action research could be a vehicle to teacher empowerment, and improved teaching and learning in the classroom. I practiced action research myself in my own teaching, incorporating what I learned each quarter into my next quarter's classes. I knew, however, that in order for me to do action research that was rigorous and valid for my practice, I had to be organized and detailed about collecting data and documenting the various things I wanted to know about my teaching.

Such organization and data collection takes time—time that many classroom teachers may feel they don't have. However, to my surprise and delight, Cathy immediately expressed excitement at the idea, and began talking about how she could set up the elements of the program, and how she could incorporate the programming into her "pull-out" sessions with children, making me feel somewhat embarrassed for my lack of zeal in promoting action research as a viable way to improve teaching and learning.

Cathy: Little did Linnea realize that while I was outwardly expressing enthusiasm, inwardly, I also felt tentative. When Linnea first suggested an action research project, my verbal words indicated that I was in complete agreement. But I was thinking, "Research? I am not really a research type of person. I hope this doesn't involve a lot of time." As I was silently talking myself out of the idea, Linnea somehow instinctively knew that I was worrying about the time commitment, and offered reassurance to ease my fears by talking about what the scope of the project might look like.

What I really found exciting was that when I proposed the idea to Laurel, the 2nd grade teacher with whom I worked, she expressed enthusiasm, saying she was "on board" for her entire classroom, and not just the seven students I was trying to help.

Laurel: I may have outwardly expressed enthusiasm, but I, too, was inwardly nervous. The idea of using my students' progress for a research project sounded great. But I initially had flashbacks to my graduate-level educational statistics course, and I got a little anxious.

However, since I am always looking for new ways to differentiate instruction in an effort to meet the needs of all students—my high-achieving students, my students who perform at grade level, and my students who are learning disabled, or at risk—I agreed when Cathy asked if I would be willing to help implement the literacy program. Cathy also suggested that we use the action research project as our alternative evaluation for the school year, an idea that I found appealing since it meant a new approach to a somewhat tedious evaluation process. And Cathy told me about Linnea's willingness to support us throughout the scope of the project, an idea that was both appealing, since it meant having an expert on board, and intimidating, since I hadn't been observed by a university faculty member in quite a number of years. After chewing this over, I agreed and decided to include the whole class because I wanted all students to experience the benefits of the project.

LAUNCHING THE PROJECT

Cathy: As a special education teacher, I am always looking for new and interesting ways to give my students an opportunity to close their achievement gap. When I attended a conference on teaching word study, I knew this was a program I wanted my students to be able to use to improve their reading and writing. Laurel has always been open to new ideas, but I was a little worried that launching an entirely new spelling program that was outside our district curriculum might be expecting too much. When I first approached her about the idea of engaging in an action research project using word study, I suggested we conduct the research using only my students with IEPs. I should have known better, because as soon as I suggested we do an action research project with our special education students, Laurel said, "Let's do it, but with my whole class!" Quite honestly, that initially seemed to be the most difficult part of the project, but in actuality it was quite easy. I think the "idea" of action research is far more daunting than actually participating in the process. Once we agreed that we were interested in working on the project, our enthusiasm continued to grow, and we came to realize that action research really didn't impose more work and time on us as teachers. The only extra demand imposed was that we had to collaboratively reflect on what we were doing and how it affected our students. But we eventually discovered that this collaborative reflection strengthened our future actions as teachers.

Linnea: I reviewed the curriculum materials that Cathy and Laurel provided and wrote a brief, 2-page proposal for the project that they gave to their principal and curriculum director. The project was approved, and Cathy and Laurel began preparing the materials for implementing the new literacy program. Laurel had a challenge in deciding how many literacy groups to prepare, as the program encouraged differentiation for each student according to their level. However, Laurel and Cathy soon realized that four to five groups would be a more feasible number to work with, and began grouping the children into developmental levels.

HOW THIS PROJECT CHANGED US AND OUR PERCEPTIONS OF ACTION RESEARCH

Reflection is considered by many authors to be essential to the action research process. But reflection is defined in different ways, and is often placed at diverse points along the action research cycle. In discussing reflection in general, Pine (2009) stated that reflecting on our practice is "required" and "eventually leads to understanding and the teacher's construction of new knowledge" (p. 179). We reflect on ourselves, and on how our perspectives of each other and of the process of action research changed, because we feel this might, in turn, encourage other novice researchers to go ahead and "give it a try." Mertler (2012) encouraged novice researchers to reflect, defining reflection as "the act of critically exploring what you are doing, why you decided to do it, and what its effects have been" (p. 14). We offer our reflections here as an example of the benefits of reflective practice, which may go far beyond the original "problem statement" or intent of the action research project.

Linnea: I credit Cathy and Laurel's combined enthusiasm and professionalism with changing my views about promoting action research. I've always believed that learning the "nuts and bolts" of action research—what some might call "book learning"—is very different from actually engaging in an action research project. But in the past I was much more hesitant to promote this approach. When teachers told me in the past that they didn't have time to do action research, I would secretly say to myself, "But if you just did the project, it would be in place of (not in addition to) your regular planning, and you would come out with tangible results that would empower you, and help you create more powerful learning environments." However, I would NEVER have said such a statement out loud to a teacher, out of respect for their own understanding and practice of their profession. Now, I think I might; and I would add, "Let me help you through the process."

I began to see how I can help teachers by offering gentle encouragement, research methods guidance, writing support, and exhortation, while also giving more respect to the value of enthusiasm and how contagious it can be within a school environment. In my own practice I continue to discuss what happened to the three of us in this project in order to provide a model for future teachers and/or veteran teachers with whom I work.

Cathy: It had a tremendous effect on me when Linnea came out to the school and took time to examine students' work/assessment samples, met personally with Laurel and me in our work environment, attended faculty meetings and a literacy program workshop, and explained and helped with the action research process. Linnea didn't just tell us what to do; rather, she took an active role as she facilitated our work in the classroom!

Although I was intimidated at first, my participation in the action research project gave me a new sense of confidence as a professional. I learned that as teachers we really all have the tools we need to examine and reflect upon our practice daily. Today's schools require data collection as part of Response to Intervention (RTI). Our schools expect that we will examine scores on a multitude of assessments to make decisions for our students. It only makes sense that a thoughtful teacher uses these scores to examine current or prospective teaching to self-evaluate our instruction.

Overall, this project taught me that action research should be a part of my daily teaching. It isn't an enormous task ... it is a useful, purposeful, easily incorporated guide to self-reflection. I will continue to use action research throughout the remainder of my career.

Laurel: Working in this project strengthened my confidence in the instruction I was delivering in the classroom. As an added bonus, I enjoyed presenting the findings from this project to other educators at an annual practitioner research forum at a nearby university, as well as to district and regional colleagues in my field. This project provided us with a vehicle for positive change in our district and in their school. It also changed each of us.

FINAL THOUGHTS

Action research may sound daunting, but we want to suggest to you that it doesn't have to be. Participating collaboratively can help you take a closer look at what you do and how you do it. It can help you build your effectiveness as a teacher, and can offer concrete results about student achievement. The work also helped build our confidence in using action research to guide our instruction, and it helped to create positive change in our building.

Action research provided us with a framework (Pine, 2009) for understanding ourselves and how working together in a collaborative action research project changed us. The main conceptual guide that helped us formulate these reflections is a belief that action research is *formalized reflection*. Pine referred to this as "dialogical validity"—that is, the extent to which the research "encouraged and generated a critical dialogue" (p. 86). Each of us learned new things about ourselves and our practice. We reiterate our main finding from this process: Action research can seem daunting, but the benefits far outweigh any time commitments we thought might encumber us.

WORKS CITED

Mertler, C. A. (2012). *Action research: Improving schools and empowering educators.* Thousand Oaks, CA: Sage.

Pine, G. J. (2009). *Teacher action research: Building knowledge democracies.* Thousand Oaks, CA: Sage.

CHAPTER THREE

Do I Really Want iPads? How Critical Questions ABOUT A School Reform Can Drive Action Research

MARGIT BOYESEN

> And the day came when the risk to remain tight in a bud was more painful than the risk it took to blossom.
>
> —ANAIS NIN

At the beginning of the year my school district embarked on the journey of ushering learning into the 21st century, and my class was selected to pilot one-to-one iPads for the lower elementary school (K–3). My partner teacher and I teach a multiage class of 44 1st, 2nd, and 3rd graders, and, for us, embarking on this one-to-one journey was not about flashy apps, but about good instruction and kids using various apps as a tool to enhance learning.

As a teacher who has immersed herself in technology for over a decade, attended conferences and workshops, and even presented at computer conferences on how to effectively incorporate technology practices into the classroom, I was excited to embark on this journey. When the iPads arrived in their tidy, sleek, white and silver boxes on September 1, 2012, I was thrilled, but admittedly a bit skeptical as well. Not the kind of skepticism that raises a judgmental eyebrow or says it can't be done, but the type that asks questions in order to seek the best possible outcome. Dictionary.com defines a skeptic as (1) "a person who questions the validity or authenticity of something purporting to be factual" and (2) "a person who maintains a doubting attitude, as toward values, plans, statements, or the character of others." My skepticism fit the first definition of questioning. It wasn't that I doubted the iPad would benefit students; I wasn't sure *how* iPads would revolutionize my teaching, and—more importantly—how they would improve the learning of the bright minds in my classroom. I wanted learning with the iPads to be purposeful—quality of instruction over quantity of apps.

In addition to my kind of skepticism, I had parents who were concerned about the iPads being just "screen time" in the classroom, causing these young learners to miss out on valuable and formative social interactions in the classroom. At Back-to-School Night, as we started to explain how the iPads would support the learning and engage the learner, the hands went up. One. Two. Fifteen. It was suddenly a lot warmer in this tiny classroom filled with more than 40 parents. The first parent begged us not to use headphones. The second parent begged us not to use the iPads, period. He didn't "believe in using technology with kids this age." Though not all the parents shared the no-daily-tech-device-for-my-kids stance, it was clear as the questions continued that many were concerned. The parents' type of skepticism was more aligned with the second definition: "a person who maintains a doubting attitude. ..."

After getting over the initial shock of the parents' response, we realized that much of their skepticism was coming from fear ... fear that their child wouldn't get the basics, fear that their hearing would be damaged, fear of the iPad being used only for playing games, fear of the unknown. The unknown *is* a scary place; it was time to actively move beyond fear—both theirs and ours—and take action in the form of research.

As classroom teachers, teacher leaders, and active members of our local affiliate of the National Writing Project, my teaching partner and I have long viewed ourselves as action researchers. We see AR as a way to grapple with challenges we encounter in the classroom through a systematic process of inquiry. We knew that for this project, framing our skepticism about the iPad adoption in the form of an AR investigation would allow us to understand the real impacts of the adoption and to hone our teaching practices to best respond to this new learning tool. Additionally, AR provides us with a vehicle to communicate about our work with other educators and position our experiences within a larger K–12 context. With one-to-one iPad and mobile device models being piloted in our own district and rapidly being adopted throughout the country, we recognized that by using AR to consider what was happening in our individual classrooms we could make a contribution to the larger conversation and potentially make a difference in the lives of teachers and children beyond our classroom walls.

Our AR question emerged: Do iPads change students' learning experience? What is gained? What is lost? We wanted the iPads to be more than flashy technology. We wanted them to also be a tool to provide differentiated learning—helping students to increase critical thinking, communication, collaboration, and creativity. To do the pilot program justice, we wanted the iPads to become tools to increase learning for our 6-, 7-, and 8-year-olds, not just to repackage old practices in new, sleek technology.

My review of the research literature revealed both successes in the classroom and cautionary tales about student access to online resources. The research revealed that students were able to successfully use the iPads as learning tools to navigate apps, do research, work collaboratively, and free up the teacher to work with individual students. I wasn't convinced the research findings definitively proved that the use of the iPads improved student learning. In addition, I wasn't finding much about iPads with younger students, and what I did find was structured around several-students-to-one-iPad ratios. My lit review findings allowed me to refine my question further: Do iPads change the learning experience of 6-, 7-, and 8-year-olds? Does the ability to access learning apps, do research, and work collaboratively help students learn more effectively than without the iPads, and would it help students to take greater ownership of their learning? The skeptic in me—the one who questions and researches—secretly wasn't sure that this definition of increasing learning would be achieved. It was time to structure (and possibly restructure) my methodology.

One of the first projects we implemented was with the 3rd graders. In October, with the presidential election coming up in November, we talked about democracy and patriotism. We read picture books and discussed the freedoms we as Americans are afforded and the fact that not everyone around the world has the freedoms we so often take for granted. Students then used the iPads to write reflections about why they're lucky to live in the United States. Since "a picture is worth a thousand words," students added a visual element to strengthen the impact of their opinions.

This was the first time students created a writing-based project directly on the iPads without prewriting in their writer's notebooks first, and as a researcher I was interested in the outcome. Reviewing both their work and our observations, we found that their writing was effective, and students were able to navigate well enough that the technology didn't get in the way of their writing. In addition, students were highly motivated to create a project that would accurately convey what they wanted to say. This became one of my early data points. However, knowing that the success of one project does not validate the iPads as successful tools to increase learning, I wondered if the 1st and 2nd graders would also be able to move beyond navigation to actually improve their communication.

The next phase of investigation took us in a slightly different direction than the original AR question had suggested. The findings didn't prove that iPads increase communication, but we did notice how the iPads were naturally supporting differentiation in the classroom and allowed innate leaders to emerge. This became a mid-year data point to support the inquiry about iPads making learning more effective. Our district has a site license for an effective math program that allows students to work at their skill level, tracks student progress, provides levels within strands for each math standard, and allows teachers to print progress reports. In launching this program, we first showed the students how to navigate within the program. As students eagerly plugged in their headphones, the normal chatter and buzz of excitement that comes with trying something new permeated the classroom. What we found was that natural leaders emerged during this activity; it wasn't just the older students helping the younger ones (which is part of the philosophy and outcome of multiage learning), it was those who understood how to navigate helping struggling students. Whereas we had already encouraged cross-age articulation and mentoring, we hadn't seen the level of mentoring we had been hoping for until we launched this math program. Now we didn't need to say, "Please talk at your table to discuss ..."—it was happening naturally. After everyone who needed help had benefitted from a student mentor showing them how, a blanketed hush settled over the classroom as all students engaged in using the math skills to earn a medal for their first strand at their level. Though the skeptic in me was gaining evidence for the power of iPads to revolutionize learning, it was still early; not all students had demonstrated the impact, and we had not seen evidence in all content areas.

Three months in we were confident that students could use the technology, that the technology was maintaining engagement, and that the iPads allowed for differentiation and leadership opportunities, but our central research question remained unanswered—were students really learning more with this technology? Identifying clear evidence of the impact on learning was challenging. This was not a design experiment with a control group; we couldn't separate the impact of the iPads from the other teaching and learning experiences in our class.

To help answer our central question, the next data entry point came when I had my advanced readers use the iPads to construct opinion writing in response to literature and post them on www.edmodo.com. Edmodo is a social media tool with which students can comment on each other's postings (we had chosen to keep our class pages closed, rather than as a public forum). One of my students, whom I shall call Ben (not his real name), had been a reluctant writer since he came to us in 1st grade; he often wrote the minimum to get by, rarely writing to his ability, and his writing was riddled with so many convention errors, it was hard to decipher the meaning at times. After reading *The Waterfall* by Jonathan London, I posed these questions to the group: "Is it a good idea to climb a waterfall? Why or why not?" After discussing the pros and cons as a class, students wrote their opinions in response to the question. It was the first time we had used the iPads to draft responses to literature, rather than start with pencil and paper. I let them know that they would be posting their opinion pieces to Edmodo and would have the opportunity to respond to each other's posts. Once students started writing, the only sound I could hear was the tapping of fingers on screens, constructing responses for and against climbing waterfalls.

To my astonishment, when the bell rang, Ben asked if he could come in at recess to finish. My reluctant writer wanted to spend his own time finishing the piece so he would have an opportunity to publish (and receive comments). I kept a smile from giving me away and just said casually, "Sure you can" in response to Ben. This was the first time he'd shown any perseverance in writing, and though my inner skeptic was in danger of dissolving, I knew that one student's interest in one assignment wasn't enough evidence. After Ben left class that afternoon, I started to look back at his work and the work of several other struggling students. I noticed that their writing on the iPad was not leaps and bounds better than other assignments, but the timeframe within which they had constructed these effective opinion pieces was a great deal shorter than when I had them write in their notebooks, and the spelling was better because of the auto-correct feature. In previous years, before our one-to-one iPads, I would not have done this activity due to time constraints, since our screen time would have included working on the desktop computers in the computer lab for 30 minutes per week. The iPads now allowed students the opportunity to write on demand, any hour of the day, any day of the week. This led me to wonder just how proficient they would become in crafting opinion pieces given this regular and frequent practice.

The skeptic in me had asked at the onset of my research if the iPads would improve communication. I also didn't want the iPads to fully replace writing on paper since developmentally, students in this age group need to practice writing with a pencil. So, maintaining a research stance, over the next few weeks we continued to have students both write in their writer's notebooks and use the iPads. Eventually, we gave the students a choice of whether they wanted to handwrite or type on the iPads, and a majority of the students chose the iPads.

Once we started seeing natural mentors emerge, increased motivation, and a desire to write and publish, we started connecting the dots and planning lessons that allowed the iPad to become a tool for synthesis and creativity. Good teaching remains at the core of any successful learning experience in the classroom, but when students have authentic learning opportunities—and the tools to create evidence of their learning—it transforms the experience. Taking a skeptic's stance in designing my action research project and iPad implementation was an important part of my learning—strengthening my understanding and practice as a teacher and ensuring that the focus of the implementation remained consistently on student learning. My partner and I embarked on this one-to-one journey with the goal that it was not about flashy apps, but about good instruction and apps as a tool to enhance learning. After creating a community of digital learners and writers, incorporating the device as a learning tool across the curriculum, and delving into blogging, the skeptic in me who was willing to ask questions in order to seek the best possible outcome is glad that I chose to take a research stance in response to concerns about this adoption. It helped me to thoughtfully and systematically respond to the challenge of introducing iPads in the classroom, and honed the use of the devices to make my teaching stronger. This is only the beginning, and we will continue to build a community of 21st-century learners with the skills to use iPads to enhance learning. I feel confident that by continuing to take on the role of action researcher, my teaching will further evolve with the use of these devices.

CHAPTER FOUR

Building ON Success

Recalling the Past to Inspire Action Research in a New Context

JOHANNA SIMKO

INSPIRATION AMPLIFICATION: FINDING MY OWN UNIQUE SPIN

As our research course instructor began describing the process of identifying a focus for our action research, I was filled with excitement—this was why I had decided to come to graduate school. I loved the opportunity to really own this work, to choose a topic that would respond to the needs of my school and allow me to grow personally and professionally. I left class that evening flooded with ideas, but soon realized that I was lacking direction. Countless nights of staring at my bedroom ceiling, thinking through a hundred different action research options, left me exhausted. If you knew me you'd know that I have a tendency to overthink, that this was not the first time I found myself staring at my ceiling. I spent too many nights listening to my alarm clock lull me to sleep with the sound of waves crashing on the beach. I was doing my best to trick my brain into turning off, it needed to rest … but this strategy stopped working as flashbacks of my professor discussing work of value, work of impact, work that matters, work that's beautiful consumed me …

It occurred to me that part of the problem resulted from being asked to think as a school leader. I've been a classroom teacher for the past 10 years and have become pretty adept at reflecting and framing questions as a teacher. But now, as a Leading School's Candidate at High Tech High's Graduate School of Education, my action research had to extend beyond the classroom. To date, I had been asked only to research and think as a teacher, now I was being asked to think as a school leader.

Finally, after one particularly restless evening, a recollection of something that my action research instructor said broke through. *This should be a passion, a task that is exciting!* I had been thinking of action research as having to try something brand new. But it now occurred to me that AR can start with implementation of an idea that is not new, but would be new on that campus, new to that teacher, new to these students. I was reminded of my first year as a student teacher when my master teacher said "Great teachers borrow each other's ideas and implement them with their own unique spin." With these wise words congealing in my brain, a simple question surfaced: What have I always dreamed of doing? The answer clicked.

FLASHBACK: AN EARLY SUCCESS

Several years earlier, after returning from an extended maternity leave to a large comprehensive urban high school, I came into an unfamiliar and somewhat uncomfortable situation. Although I had originally been hired to teach English, that position was no longer available, and I found myself assigned to be a full-time theater teacher. Technically, I was qualified to teach theater—highly qualified, in fact, under the terms of No Child Left Behind, but the reality was much different; I really didn't know what I was doing. Fortunately, I found inspiration in a neighboring classroom that was the site of the school's peer counseling and mentorship program. I had noticed multiple times that this classroom functioned as a student hub; students weren't in seats but were usually in and out the door. They were trusted to work in locations around school where they weren't under the direct supervision of a teacher; they were largely on task and motivated. It occurred to me that although the missions of the peer mentor and theater programs were quite different, what needed to be done to ensure their success was very similar. My goal became to get my theater production students operating as these student mentors were. I figured that with the great responsibility that was being given to them, a culture of mutual respect and trust was going to be essential. Compelled to learn how to cultivate this culture within my theater program, I began to investigate.

A few weeks later I launched a mentorship program within the theater program. My more advanced students began to mentor my beginning students. The students themselves were given increased responsibility for driving the theater productions. I moved from being the director to being the coach, allowing the students themselves to take over responsibilities for theater design, stage direction, and production. I mentored my advanced students in their work and they, in turn, mentored the beginning and intermediate classes. Together we created some amazing productions, and it became readily apparent that when students are asked to behave as "adults" to complete a task that is of interest and value to them, their true capabilities are revealed.

Even in these early days I had visions that this approach could be expanded. I loved the success that I'd seen for my theater students, but what about the other students, the ones not enrolled in a theater class or the peer mentorship program? Would other students benefit from being involved in similar work? How could we move from an individual class to a schoolwide program? These questions led to a dream of something bigger, but the pressures of time and the limitations of my role as a classroom teacher meant that for many years, that dream remained dormant.

FLASH FORWARD: A NEW SPIN

But now, with the encouragement of a supportive principal at a new school, as well as the impetus of an action research requirement, that dream resurfaced. What have I always dreamed of doing? That was the question that evolved from my restless nights, and once framed in this way, the answer became obvious—I would start a schoolwide mentorship program and investigate its impact on students, teachers, and school culture.

Once I had identified my focus, I began to do some preliminary needs assessment work. During an observation of a colleague who teaches 9th grade, I looked around the classroom and thought about the supports available for our 9th grade students. I began thinking ... *When they are failing their classes, who do they go to? When their parents divorce, their grades are failing, or their "best friend" just told someone a hurtful untruth, who do they go to? What happens when they have something they want to say, but aren't sure who to say it to?* These 9th grade students could benefit from developing relationships with mentors. At the same time, I recognized that my own 12th grade students would benefit from the opportunity to develop leadership skills and mentor students who were slightly younger than themselves. My action research focus began to take shape—I could research and create on campus a program to train junior and senior students who would be ready, willing, and able to take on the task of mentoring freshmen students.

CONNECTING INSPIRATIONS

Often, AR is thought of as a way to solve a problem. Some of the AR textbooks even tell you that the first step in designing your research is to identify a problem. For me, the genesis of my AR came not from a present-day problem but from a past success.

Action research is a reflection of what you hold close as a practitioner. It is an opportunity to do something that you've long dreamed of, a chance to show what you value, what you want to contribute, what you want to learn more about. It's turning research into impactful action.

CHAPTER FIVE

My Journey TOWARD A Workable Action Research Question

QUDSIA KALSOOM

I vividly remember my first experience of framing an action research question. I was taking a course on action research, and we were asked to identify a research problem to pursue as a part of the course. I eagerly started working on my action research project, carefully following the steps discussed in literature on action research. I began by brainstorming problems I observed in my classroom, which focused my attention on the theme of students' dependence on me to meet small challenges: solving puzzles, developing puzzles, recording observations in science experiments, resolving conflicts, deciding on classroom rules, etc. As a next step, I tried to figure out the reasons for this dependence by asking myself a series of questions. Is this because of students' attitudes? Do I really appreciate students' decisions? Do I give my students tasks requiring responsibility? Reflecting on this trail of questions, I realized that I rarely gave students tasks that required self-direction, and yet I expected it of them. This process helped me to identify a potential cause of the problem (and how I might be contributing to it), and recognize early on the importance of reflection to the action research process.

Once I had identified a potential cause to the dilemma I wanted to address, I started reading educational literature around teaching and learning methods to find a possible solution. I discovered many ways to place responsibility with students, but gravitated toward the project method (or project-based learning) and decided to investigate the usefulness of this method with my 8th grade students. My research question was: How do projects make pupils independent learners? This question seemed perfect to me. It had an explicit action (i.e., projects) and a clear goal (i.e., independent learners)—both being useful elements in an action research question.

I took the question to my supervisor excitedly for a discussion. She said, "Good thought! Do you know the answer to this question?" I said, "Yes. I have read a lot of literature about project method and it has been reported that projects help in making pupils autonomous learners." My supervisor smiled and said that if the answer was already there in the literature, then why would I like to investigate it again? I said that I wanted to try it with my pupils and see if it could work in my class. She said, "Very good, but then tailor your question to make it specific for you and your classroom." But how? I did not ask. Instead, I left her office confused.

To gain clarity I returned to the literature once more. How could I frame an appropriate question for my action research project? And what made a question appropriate for action research in the first place? I read texts on action research available at my university, but could not find answers to my questions. During a get-together of course mates, we talked about our research progress. I learned that everyone was struggling with her/his research project. This made me realize that uncertainty and difficulty are normal at the beginning. Talking to other novice researchers greatly relieved my tension.

A few days later, I decided to analyze research questions in action research articles to learn how action researchers frame questions. As I read, I replaced the key words in each question with the key words from my research. For example, in the question, "What happens to my students' *writing skills* when they produce *reports on classroom activities*?" I replaced "writing skills" with "independent learning skills" and "reports on class activities" with "class projects." My question began to look like: What happens to my students' *independent learning skills* when they produce *class projects*? In this way I wrote almost five questions. I found this strategy helpful in framing questions as a new researcher. I also had a discussion with a senior colleague about my question. I told her that I wanted to try out the project method with my pupils to see if they developed independent learning skills, and she advised me to include all this in my question. Now my question was: How can I use project method in my class to help develop pupils as independent learners?

Through this process, I learned that there is no single way of writing action research questions. An action research question may contain a clear action and a desired outcome, or it may explicitly state only one of these. As a beginner, I found it beneficial to include both the action and the expected outcome in my question. Clearly stating both helped me stay focused on what I would do, and what I hoped to achieve.

When I took my question back to my research supervisor, she said, "Very good! Now it looks like an action research question." I asked her that what she meant, and she explained, "It is certainly difficult to define an action research question. However, it may be taken as a question that requires investigation of an action by the researcher to solve a problem or bring a change. Medical practitioners continuously raise action research questions during their practice, like: How can I use combination of medicines A, C, and H to treat a chronic bad throat? The most important characteristic of an action research question is that it is action-oriented."

The example given by my supervisor triggered my thoughts, and I started forming different action research questions in my mind: How can I use project method to make my pupils more interested in science? What will happen to my pupils' report writing skills when I ask them to submit daily reports of their projects? What happens to my pupils' self-evaluation skills when I require them to evaluate their own projects? What happens to students' critical thinking when I ask them to construct science puzzles? How can I use brainstorming activities to scaffold my pupils' learning? How can I use real-life cases in reading comprehension classes to make my pupils aware of gender stereotypes in our society? What will happen to my students' social skills when they are asked to work in heterogeneous groups for a full term?

Here I realized that framing action research questions was in fact not very difficult. All I needed was an awareness of the issues I wanted to address, and a desire to improve. For me, it also helped to clarify the action I wanted to take and the outcome I hoped for. Below are some considerations that have helped me in phrasing questions for subsequent action research projects.

IDENTIFY A CLEAR ACTION

I found it useful to include a clear action in my question so that I had a clear direction for my next steps. A question such as "How can I improve pupils' writing skills?" could be a good starting point for digging into the literature, but once you know the actions you want to take, it helps to make them explicit in the question so you can stay focused.

SELECT A RESEARCHABLE QUESTION

Though action research is fluid, it follows a scientific method of investigation and relies on data to come to conclusions. If the answer to a question can be found by reading alone, the question is not a research question. A question like "What are different methods for improving students' writing skills?" is not a good action research question because the answer to this question is already available in educational literature. In addition, the question doesn't imply any action on your part. On the other hand, the question "How can I improve my pupils' writing skills?"

requires data. The researcher will have to live with the question—and to act—to find an answer.

FRAME YOUR ACTION NARROWLY

My experience of doing action research has taught me that broad actions can cause difficulty. The question "What happens to my students' engagement when I use activity-based teaching?" has a broad action in it (i.e., activity-based teaching). There are many activity-based teaching methods. Most likely, all of them cannot be studied in the time teachers are able to devote to research. In addition, the more specific we can be about our actions, the more precise we can be in our findings. For example, let's say that under the umbrella of "activity-based teaching" I try guided inquiry and role-playing activities in my class, and I find them useful in improving student engagement. It would be misleading to conclude that activity-based teaching methods improved student engagement. After all, I tried only two activity-based teaching methods. It would, however, be accurate (and helpful) to conclude that guided inquiry and role-playing activities improved student engagement. These are actions that are narrowly defined, which means it is easier for other teachers to learn about them and take similar actions themselves.

INCLUDE AN EXPECTED OUTCOME

The primary focus of action research is to improve something. I found that if that "something" is included in the action research question, it clarifies expectations and can help focus data collection. For example, a question like "What happens when I use Directed Activities Related to Texts (DART) activities in my class?" doesn't make clear what you want to happen, or what you want to look for evidence of. In cases like this, it can be helpful to brainstorm subquestions that highlight what you want to improve: What happens to the quality of students' writing when we use DART? To their feelings about reading? To their ability to comprehend texts? Then you can ask yourself what data you could draw upon to answer these questions. This way, by focusing on something, you can avoid the pitfall of trying to look at everything.

FRAME OPEN-ENDED QUESTIONS

Action research occurs in cycles, with no clear end or usually clear answer. The purpose is to explore different possibilities and to go deeper as one question leads to another. Research questions with yes or no answers, like "Is prompt feedback useful to develop students' writing skills?" or "Are DARTs helpful in improving pupils' comprehension?" will not lead to fruitful inquiries or continual improvement.

OWN IT

The most important characteristic of an action research question is that the researcher feels true ownership of it and is committed to acting on it. One way to do this is to make yourself visible in the question. For example, a question like "How does prompt feedback improve pupils' writing skills?" could be studied through purely experimental means. However, questions like "How can *I* give feedback that effectively supports students' writing skills?" or "What happens to my students' writing skills when *I* give them prompt feedback on their writing assignments?" require action and reflection on your part.

The whole process of developing questions for my first action research was like developing a relationship: a love affair. It started with a lot of excitement and stimulation, went through a phase of tension, uncertainty, and mistrust, and finally culminated as a passion and direction for next steps. Now, if only all love affairs ended so well!

CHAPTER SIX

Moving from "Noticings" to Research Questions

JOCELYN PECK

I was overwhelmed with topic options for action research. I knew I wanted to look into making math class a more positive experience for my high school students, but I wasn't sure which road to take. Many of the students were frustrated with math, feeling like it was disconnected from the real world. Several of them had given up, believing they were simply "bad at math," and their negativity was beginning to infect the class community as a whole. As I began the AR process, my advisor suggested that I make a list of observations about what was happening in the class. What did I notice?

- I noticed some of my students weren't persevering through their work.
- I noticed some weren't creatively attacking problems.
- I noticed many were checked out and constantly relying on the "smart kids."
- I noticed the kids were on their phones.
- I noticed I had no structure in my class to make those phones useful.
- I noticed all of these articles swarming around me about how the flipped classroom model is the new cure-all in a math class, especially for those classes in which students were struggling to complete problems for homework.

I knew if I was going to ever select a topic and be content with it, I would have to gather student input and not just rely on what I had observed. If I had relied on just my observations, it would have been difficult to understand why those things were occurring. Those "whys" are the driving forces behind the planning of action research, and they respond to an issue instead of a symptom.

If you are also in the position of feeling overwhelmed by the topic possibilities in AR, here are a few strategies that I found helped me to move from vague wonderings to a focused question around which I could build my research.

CONSIDER THE DATA YOU ALREADY HAVE

As teachers, we are constantly collecting data on our students. The tests we give, attendance we collect, and grades we issue all serve as forms of data that can be used to refine our research focus. As I moved forward with looking at bolstering my students' attitudes in my class, I reached for these data sets to determine if the things that I had noticed in my initial observations were affecting student success in my class. I looked more closely at homework completion rates among all my students, focusing in on those students who were always complaining about being "bad at math." I had expected a strong correlation between self-perception and academic scores, but that wasn't what I encountered when I looked at the data more closely. To be sure, the students with a negative self-perception had low homework and test scores, but neutral or positive self-perception did not correspond with higher scores. Looking at these data sets informed me that I needed to reach out to more of my students to gather information on the topic—no teacher is aware of all of the thoughts and feelings of his or her students, and, as a new teacher, I was probably even less aware.

As I shifted from the role of teacher to teacher researcher, I found myself looking at student data more systematically. Before beginning the process of action research, I looked at grades and a student's comments as information for supporting that individual student. With the lens of a teacher researcher, I began viewing these grades and comments in their aggregate form to gather information on supporting the class as a whole. They were no longer singular events, but clues to my underlying problem on which I needed to focus my research.

TALK TO YOUR STUDENTS

Students tend to complain about school; my students were no different. Among these complaints, though, I found more information about my noticings. The most common complaint I would hear is "This work is too hard," but one day a student elaborated further, "You didn't teach me this before I had to do it for homework, so I couldn't do it. It was too hard." I have to admit, that hurt. I knew that I had given a lesson on the material; I had answered questions and given students time in class to practice. Initially I was frustrated by what I would have previously perceived as laziness, but I was also intrigued by the student's boldness in saying I had not done my part. In talking more with the student, I found that he quickly fell back on a former excuse, "I'm not good at math," but this time he added more information, "I just need more time to learn it."

Time is a precious commodity in schools, and there is great pressure to "keep up" with the required curriculum. I thought I had found a balance between building understanding and getting through the curriculum, but as I had further conversations with students, I found that many felt that we were moving too quickly for them to master the concepts with confidence. I began to recognize student complaints as a launching point for gathering more data.

Where possible, don't ignore a complaint; brace yourself for honesty and have the student elaborate. If it seems like there is something outside of your class that is causing their complaint, it probably isn't a good basis for a research question and should not be included in your needs assessment. But if the complaint stems from a concern in class, engage in conversation to try to understand the motivating issues behind the concerns; addressing these issues can allow AR to fundamentally strengthen teaching and learning in your classroom. At times, students may also give you positive feedback on your lessons. Take advantage of these opportunities as well. Ask them what was different in the lesson? Were they more awake, well-fed, in the honeymoon phase of a new relationship, or did you actually do something differently that they connected with? Asking these questions can help you maintain your role as both teacher and researcher—you are showing your students that you care and that you are collecting useful data.

INTRODUCE NEW DATA COLLECTION TOOLS

At a certain point, you'll need to reach beyond the informal conversations and the review of data sets you've already collected to create a new needs assessment. This needs assessment should build on the ideas you've gathered through your previous data review and your conversations with students to create a more systematic snapshot of the class around your prospective focus area of research. My needs assessment was an online survey that included one scaled response ("On a scale from 1 to 10 ...") and two paragraph responses. My earlier data review had allowed me to be purposeful in my survey prompts, asking fewer questions that were more tailored to my evolving research focus. My scaled response question allowed me to determine how widespread concerns about issues of time were in the class, while my open-ended survey questions were more general, trying to ascertain some of my students' underlying concerns, with the goal of having the student responses guide me to creating a research question and action plan for supporting students who view themselves as "bad at math."

Survey questions can be difficult to craft. A few considerations that can help:

(1) Be thoughtful about how you intend to analyze the responses; thinking about this in advance will help you determine what type of questions you want to include (scaled, multiple choice, free response, etc.).
(2) Try to include a balance to forced-response and free-response questions. I found that my free-response questions provided me with the most meaningful data for creating a research question and, eventually, an action plan.
(3) The language in your questions should be clear and simple so that students require no additional explanation to make sense of the question. I had high school students at a school with lots of Internet access, so an online survey worked for me. You'll need to adjust the language and structure of your needs assessment to respond to the age of your students and the context of your school.
(4) Try to avoid leading language that will lead to insincere survey responses.

With these considerations in mind, look over a list of brainstormed questions and predict possible responses from your students. You will quickly find your list shrinking as you realize some of the questions will generate only one response, while others will be insincerely answered. Some questions may be able to be combined into one. Eventually, you should have a strong, concise list of questions that get to the root of your area of interest.

SOUND OUT POTENTIAL ACTION PLANS WITH STUDENTS

After analyzing the data from my needs assessment survey, I found myself drawn to the idea of using social media to support my action research. Student survey responses had pointed me in this direction, and it seemed like a plausible way to find more time to support math learning by engaging with them through social media outside of the classroom. Before I launched into designing the action plan, however, I wanted to get student input on the concept. I shared the idea with my students and asked for their help in identifying an appropriate social media platform. I asked them to share what social media platforms they used most frequently and to consider what would be the best medium for creating a math learning community on a social network. We sat and talked about the pros and cons of the different platforms and decided together which approach would best support our needs.

The age of my students made it very simple and rather necessary to include them in decisions on changing a classroom structure. Since this is their classroom too, including students in my action planning and decision-making process helped them to feel ownership of the potential changes I would implement, and helped me to feel confident that my ideas wouldn't run into significant resistance when I began implementation. Although the sounding-out process may look different with younger students, the basic concept of sharing ideas and asking for their feedback has resonance across grade levels. Involving students in the process and being transparent about your rationale is an important step in moving from noticings to research questions and action plans.

DON'T BE AFRAID TO MOVE IN UNEXPECTED DIRECTIONS

Data from multiple assessments consistently showed me that my students wanted more time to get help in class. However, as a relatively new teacher expected to "keep up" with my colleagues, I didn't feel that I could slow down the pacing of the course. I had to adapt and find creative ways to find "time" outside the classroom. I had originally thought that my entire action research project would take place in the classroom. I conferred with my colleagues and advisors to consider how to give my students more instructional time without taking away work time in class. Eventually I accepted that much of this intervention could not be completed in the classroom. The students who needed more time would require much more than I had to offer in class or office hours, and many of them needed specialized instruction. I decided to use a strategy I was initially skeptical of: I would use online instructional supports to give my students the additional instructional time they needed.

If you had asked me a few weeks earlier, I would never have predicted that this would have become the focus on my research. But looking at the data, talking with my students, and considering potential options clearly pointed me in this direction. And once I accepted it, my research questions became clear:

- What happens when classroom instruction is supplemented by online instruction?
- How are student attitudes about homework affected by having the additional instruction available to the students on demand?
- How does the class collaboration in gathering additional resources affect student-directed learning?
- How does the source of the additional content (student selected vs. teacher selected) impact the effect on student engagement and learning?

The needs assessment data and these early conversations with students were instrumental in focusing my research and helping me to move from my initial noticings to focused action research questions. Although the needs assessment data did not tell me what I thought I wanted to hear, it ultimately led me in a direction that significantly impacted the quality of learning and the learning community in my classroom. Taking time to review data, assess needs, and talk with students prior to launching into your AR will help you to identify the underlying concerns in your classroom and to consider potential solutions. Once these concerns and solutions emerge, your AR question will follow.

CHAPTER SEVEN

Goals, Questions, and Anxiety

Initiating the Research Process

ASHLEY VASQUEZ

To begin my research process, I had to design a research question with accompanying goals. This was more difficult than it sounds. I had all these ideas swirling in my head, each taking me to a different place. How would I be able to begin my research process when I wasn't even sure what I wanted to research? I knew I wanted to increase student engagement, motivation, and collaboration. I knew I wanted to move away from focusing on standardized testing in my classroom. I saw how my students were losing the ability to have meaningful conversations with other students, adults, and community members. I have always had a passion for service-oriented learning, and have always wanted my students to understand their impact on the world. There was also the idea of increasing parent involvement. How was I ever going to get at the heart of my research when I had all these ideas bouncing around? More importantly, how could I roll all of these ideas into one?

I began to weigh the pros and cons of each possible research idea. I thought about which ideas could be put aside for now. I began asking myself what I really wanted to accomplish. Undoubtedly, I wanted to become a better teacher. I also wanted my students to become better people. I wanted them to care about each other, help each other, and work with others. I wanted my students to be excited about learning. As I thought about all of these goals, I knew I needed to focus my research around community service learning. With community service learning, not only would my students be learning, they would be helping other people and in turn becoming better people themselves. Or so I hoped.

With goals and techniques in mind, I set out to finally design my question. I yearned to do everything right the first time. I was convinced that if I didn't get it right now, it would be more work in the future, and more time spent changing it. Time was something I didn't have.

The hardest thing for me to realize early on was that I didn't need to end world hunger with one research study. Fortunately, I soon realized that this process was just the tip of the iceberg for my growing and learning as an educator. I needed to keep it simple and manageable. I needed to let go a little and truly focus on my core goals. Once I understood this, I was able to form a research question: How do students experience community service learning in 2nd grade? With the focus on my students' experience, I wouldn't have to necessarily prove anything right or wrong. My study would be more about the growing, learning, and changing process rather than finding (or confirming) the solution to a problem.

QUESTION DONE. NOW WHAT?

With an established question, I began delving into community service learning resources. I needed some background knowledge. I needed to decide on what my structure for implementation would look like. As I searched through the work of those before me, I hit a wall. Community service learning is common in high school and college, but rarely seen at the elementary school level. How was I going to implement community service learning in my 2nd grade classroom when there was no precedence, no guidance, and no structure to follow? I needed to start collecting data in my classroom, and here I was still trying to decide how to structure it. I felt that it was too late to turn back. This resulted in a standstill, not moving forward and refusing to move back.

Was this something that I really wanted to do? With a mind full of doubt, I decided to have a few meaningful conversations with my professors and surrounding colleagues. Their positive encouragement and helpful suggestions pushed me in the right direction. They reminded me that I didn't have to structure my research in any set way or manner. I found the aspects of community service learning structures in high school and college that I liked, and I applied them to my own classroom. Sure, there were aspects that I needed to tweak and modify to accommodate a younger cohort, but I already knew that differentiation is part of any effective teaching strategy. You need to know when it works for your students and when it doesn't.

LEARNING TO REIN IT IN

With a research question, research goals, and structure of implementation, I felt that I was ready to get this process moving. This moment of clarity was short-lived. As it was when trying to design my research question, my mind began filling with numerous possible community service learning project ideas. My students were going to work with the elderly. They were going to lead a schoolwide recycling campaign. They were going to reduce waste and create a compost bin. Maybe they could start a school garden! How about tutoring for younger students? The ideas were endless.

I noticed that I was trying to end world hunger again, with the sweep of one research study. I was going overboard and I was paralyzed again, not moving forward and determined not to move back. If anything, this research process has taught me to rein it in a bit. At times I get a tad excited and consume myself with all the possibilities. Meanwhile, nothing is actually accomplished, I become discouraged, and I feel like abandoning ship. I have learned that several small steps are usually better than one giant step. The pressure of perfecting your one giant step usually prevents you from actually moving at all.

I decided to start small and see where it took me. I chose a project idea focused on fire safety and tossed it out to my students. I wanted them to have ownership in the research process and feel like they had a say in what we were doing. That being said, I initially failed to provide much guidance or structure. I was so conscientious about not controlling my students' every move in our community service learning experience that I failed to recognize where my input and leadership was needed. I didn't create a prototype or model the process—things I needed to do, considering that many, if not all, of my students had never experienced community service learning before. Students were excited and happy, but they didn't quite know what to do. I was so worried about the community service learning structure I was going to implement that I didn't realize that my students weren't ready for the complete independence I was offering them.

This helped me improve my pitch for our second project, which was focused on helping children at the local children's hospital. I saw that my students needed a balance between choice and teacher facilitation. I set some key parameters and let students choose their roles and responsibilities. As a result, students were far more productive and independent. They didn't need to spend so much time asking for additional explanation.

The research experience revealed to me the importance of striking a balance between teacher and student control in classroom activities. Ultimately, it wasn't even the structure of our projects that ended up mattering most. With key components built in, such as a designated audience, opportunities for student collaboration, and time to reflect, community service learning was a successful and useful experience no matter what proven and previously studied structure I put in place.

In regards to data collection, I strived to do it all. I was the determined researcher armed with interviews, surveys, exit cards, observations, journals, videos, and anything else you could think of. The problem was that 2nd grade students require a lot of your time … time I didn't have to spend on my list of 20 data collection methods.

In reality, I ended up relying on class discussions, surveys, a few exit cards, and student journals to fuel my research. I found my students' journals to be incredibly useful. By frequently writing in their journals throughout the process, my students were able to see themselves grow as writers and thinkers. I was able to see how far they had come in their abilities to reflect and critically think about community service learning. As we progressed through our community service learning projects, my students became more enthused and excited, writing longer and more fluent sentences. My students' journals helped me manage my data collection. At any moment, I could open up a student journal and see what they were thinking at a specific moment in the research process, even if it was 2 months past. My students' journals helped me catch many of those moments I might have otherwise missed. They also helped me identify a finding that I hadn't anticipated: that community service learning can help students develop as writers by giving them something they are eager to write about.

PROVING VS. EXPERIENCING

When I set out to do this study, I had a secret agenda. I wanted to prove that young students were capable of doing complex activities such as community service learning. I had become conscious of the fact the many people (educators, parents, administrators) had limited expectations of young students. Many believe that 7-year-olds are unable to develop meaningful relationships with community members, aren't mature enough to develop and express empathy, and have difficulty engaging in reflective and critical thinking. I have always had high expectations of my students, and I wanted everyone else to as well. I wanted my colleagues to see that complex strategies such as community service learning and project-based learning were possible at any age.

Ironically, as I began my action research, I too wondered if my students would be able to succeed with my goals. I worried about failing. Maybe my students were too young. In my preoccupation and determination, I wasn't listening to my students. Who knew better than the students themselves whether or not they could do something? With a research question focused around student experience, I was able to let my students' voices guide me through the research process. And by focusing on telling *our* story, rather than proving or disproving a hypothesis, I was able to concentrate my energy on doing everything in my power to make community service learning a success. As a result, I learned much about what works and what doesn't in doing this work with young children, and I was able to keep students' voices front and center in my findings.

Looking at the big picture, the research process impacted everyone involved, but most importantly, it impacted me. I have evolved as an educator. I have evolved as a person. I have learned to let go of perfection. This doesn't mean I have stopped dreaming big dreams. It means I am okay with making little changes and taking smaller steps to make those dreams a reality. I've come to terms with finding happiness in the little accomplishments, because when you add all the little accomplishments together, you have one big accomplishment. I've learned to give my students more control—not complete control, but more control. My students have shown me that they need me to provide some support and structure, but they are more than willing to manage the rest. Most importantly, I have learned to listen. I used to spend a good amount of time telling my students how they should learn and what they should learn. Now I let my students' thoughts, ideas, and voices guide my instruction. When my students know they are being listened to, they are more enthusiastic and motivated learners. What more could I ask for?

SECTION TWO

Designing Action Research

> Action research is demanding, complex and challenging because the researcher not only assumes responsibilities for doing the research but also for enacting change. Enacting change is not easy—it requires time, patience, and sound planning …
>
> —PINE, 2009, PP. 234–235

So, you have your research question. You've identified what you want to improve. You've had a few interesting conversations with colleagues and advisors about your ideas, and perhaps even started to dig into the literature on your topic. Now what?

This is the moment that trips many of us up. We start to wonder what types of data will help us explore our question, how to analyze that data so that we can pull some useful meaning from it, and how to integrate data collection and analysis methods into our everyday practice so that it informs our decisions and our actions (and doesn't make us feel schizophrenic in the process).

The good news is that we educators collect and analyze data every day, and use it to inform our practice, whether we are aware of it or not. We constantly observe what is going on, who is doing what, and when they do it. We sift through documents, artifacts of student learning, and students' reflections on their progress. We ask students questions and engage them in conversations, sometimes individually and sometimes in groups. We modify our instruction on a daily, sometimes hourly basis based on what we have learned about the students in our care and what will best meet their needs.

Action research, then, is an extension of what you are already doing, though in a more systematic and focused way. It is an opportunity to be thoughtful about what we most want to accomplish for our students and ourselves, and to orient our efforts—our reading, data collection, sense-making, decisions, and actions—toward those goals.

A key part of this process is the research design. Teacher action research is unique in that it is both research and an intervention. We are active and influential participants in the contexts we study, and we hope that our actions will have a positive impact on our students. We are not impartial observers, but active users of the knowledge we generate. As a result, our research design includes both the actions we will take and the data we will collect and analyze, and each informs the other.

Hubbard and Power refer to the research plan, or research design, as the "backbone for your study—a skeletal frame on which to hang all your emerging thoughts about your research question, data collection, and how you might sustain your research" (1999, p. 47). Like all good plans, the research design provides a helpful foundation to return to when life gets busy. It reminds us what we thought was most important to pay attention to, and can help us focus our energy (and our data collection) in constructive ways. And paradoxically, committing to the thinking it takes to create a research design usually means we are able to thoughtfully deviate from it when we need to, as Bryan Meyer discusses in chapter 9.

Pine notes, "Action research takes place in a context of discovery and invention as opposed to a context of verification" (2009, p. 236). Discovery and invention can be messy, uncomfortable, and exhilarating. The research plan helps us stay committed to the discovery process, and reminds us that action research is iterative, with each cycle informing the next. In our own work, we've found the following questions helpful to ponder when crafting a research design: What do I want to improve? What do I need to understand more deeply to make improvements? What data will I collect, and how will I make sense of it, to gain this understanding? Based on what I learn, what action will I take? How will I know if these actions have been effective or not? And finally, what will I do next as a result?

In the following chapters, teacher researchers share reflections on the process of developing and implementing a research design, and the varied sources of inspiration they found along the way.

Juli Ruff chronicles her journey through the literature, and makes the case that the literature review can be one of the most valuable and lasting parts of the action research process if it is approached as a "living breathing beast" that continues to evolve and guide our next steps. She offers practical advice about how to engage with the literature, and with our own experiences, in ways that are authentic and meaningful.

Bryan Meyer discusses how his research design and methods evolved over time as he developed a deeper understanding of both the concept he was studying and his students. While his initial research design provided a launching point, Bryan reflects on the ways he adapted many of his research "tools" to help him unearth multiple perspectives and dig into "critical observations" as they unfolded.

Bernice Alota addresses a common concern among teachers in general and teacher researchers in particular: time. In our classrooms, where we often feel that there is too much to do and not enough time to do it, how do we find the time to "squeeze in" the additional task of action research? Bernice encourages teacher researchers to view AR not as a separate element in the classroom, but as another lens through which to view our day-to-day work. She offers practical suggestions for building action and assessment plans that fit into our existing classroom structures and also open up the space for real learning and reflection to take place.

Sarah Strong focuses her chapter on data collection methods. She offers practical suggestions for creating data collection methods that are both sustainable and directly relevant to our work with students. She discusses how her own data collection methods became her most effective forms of formative assessment, and how she came to see her own experience as an essential source of data worth reflecting on, analyzing, and sharing.

Cady Staff reminds us that stories are powerful teachers, and that the stories we want to tell can drive our research design in powerful ways. In Cady's case, her fascination with how students worked together led her to conduct case studies of teams. Along the way, she learned to recognize and let go of the stories she wanted to tell when she began, and found ways to open herself up to the stories students wanted to tell, engaging them as collaborators in shaping their collective story.

Finally, Steve Hamilton argues that action research is inherently good research, though traditional notions of validity, replicability, and generalizability may not apply. Instead, he proposes that rigor resides in the degree to which action research serves an authentic purpose in the local context—meaning, that it informs effective action and ultimately yields the intended results. He also offers advice about how to check our own assumptions throughout our research so that our results are trustworthy, as all good research should be.

Questions to ponder as you read these chapters and think about your own work:

- What researchers, theorists, and practitioners are guiding your thinking about your research question and your design—both the actions you might take and possible data collection and analysis methods? What "sticky" points are emerging as themes across this work?
- What are your goals for students and for your own practice? What might these look/sound/feel like in practice? What data collection and analysis methods would allow you to explore if your goals were being met or not?
- How can your data collection and analysis methods be integrated into your everyday practice of teaching and learning?

- What is the story you want to tell? How will you remain open to other stories as well? And how could your research design support you in telling the stories that are most true?
- Do case studies or focus students have a place in your own work? How might you select a diverse set of cases/students to provide multiple perspectives?
- How can you involve students and colleagues as collaborators in your research and as "checks" on your own interpretations?

WORKS CITED

Hubbard, R., & Power, B. (1999). *Living the questions: A guide for teacher-researchers.* York, ME: Stenhouse Publishers.

Pine, G. (2009). *Teacher action research: Building knowledge democracies.* Thousand Oaks, CA: Sage Publications.

CHAPTER EIGHT

Taming THE Beast

Researching and Writing a Literature Review

JULI RUFF

I have a friend who loves to do research. And I mean RESEARCH. There is nothing she finds more titillating than sitting in a library, delving through articles in her chosen field. It excites her. But that is not me. I would rather be running or jumping or fishing or digging outside.

When it came to the part of my action research when I was supposed to be poring over articles and looking into all the things others have learned, I was less than excited. Whether you call the section a "Lit Review" or your evolving "Understandings," I knew the reality of what needed to happen included many hours of sitting still, reading, and writing. In addition to being incredibly overwhelming, it also sounded a bit boring. Not really my cup of tea.

That is why I think it is startling that completing this aspect of my action research remains one of the most rewarding parts of the process for me. It is the part that bridged the gap between the teacher I was for 12 or so years and the teacher I had always wanted to become. Of all the many steps in the action research process, it is the one that caused my teaching to change the most—not just how I present this or that procedure, or what sort of things I teach in what progression, but the entire framework and philosophy for how I approach each day with each student. It also gave me faith that I could change my classroom and improve in ways I had long since stopped trying, because I simply thought it was beyond my ability. Most importantly, though, it is the part of my research write-up that I actually go back and reread regularly. It has become a regular tool for me, pushing me to question both why I do a lot of what I do, and also the value of things I always felt I should do, like writing comments all over students' essays or offering students advice.

Old habits die hard, and I often find myself falling into my old ways. Let's face it, I like to talk and offer my opinions, even to students. Rereading my review of others' research reminds me of not only what I learned, but also, and more importantly for me, the philosophical underpinnings of why it is important and worth my constant thought and consideration. I don't write many comments on students' papers anymore, and I purposely try not to offer advice or my opinions to students. Instead, I facilitate ways for students to get feedback from each other on their work, and to self-reflect on it as well. This is a direct result of articles I read that made me think about how having a teacher (who inherently has the most power in the room) can actually inhibit student thinking. Because of my work on my lit review and the articles I read, I step back more in class, keep myself out of the center of lessons, and generally have more faith in my students. While I was reading and writing, I was not just synthesizing other people's ideas. I was in dialogue with them, reflecting on what they made me think and wonder, and how their work might influence what I did in my classroom and for my action research.

But no matter how worthwhile it was, it was also incredibly daunting. At least I thought so. Looking back, however, there are some lessons I learned that made it easier for me to delve into the research, even as a reluctant, overwhelmed and under-experienced novice researcher.

LESSON 1: LEARN TO READ WHAT YOU WANT, NOT WHAT YOU FEEL YOU SHOULD

Maybe this seems obvious, but it wasn't for me. When I came to the point when my master's program required that I start sifting through articles, I felt like there were a bunch of things I should do or should read. It felt like I was supposed to achieve something specific or prove something exact. No matter how many times my professors told me that wasn't the case, it was still the feeling that weighed on me. The weight became so heavy that I think I emotionally broke and just decided it was so difficult, and I was so convinced I'd probably fail at it anyway, that I decided I wasn't going to do it. Instead, I was just going to read what interested me. If I was doomed to fail at the larger project, I might as well not be bored in the process.

To start, I asked mentors for reading suggestions. I asked my professors, I asked my graduate school peers, and I asked my teaching colleagues. Because I had asked so many people, they soon started coming up on their own and offering suggestions that made them think of me. In the end, these were my favorite reads. I also went to the library and found an article that loosely related to my research topic and seemed interesting. I liked it, so I read something else by the same person. I liked that one, so I looked at who that author had read, and read some of that stuff, even though it did not seem to directly relate to my topic. When a friend told me about a good book, I read it, even if it didn't really seem to apply. I even picked up some John Dewey, just because everybody always talks about him and I figured, what the heck. I ended up using all of these sources in my write-up of related literature. It turned out that what was interesting also applied to my work.

LESSON 2: WHEN IN DOUBT, CHOOSE DEPTH IN YOUR READING

I can think of only one article I read that I felt was a waste of time. I had been reading full articles that were each 40 or so pages of dense but informative research. Because of this, I was having a tough time keeping up with the two articles we were supposed to read each week, and became overwhelmed by the amount of time it took me to read. Someone in my class who looked much less stressed about the reading load told me about these great little professional journals with 5-page articles that were basically the shortened write-ups from someone's larger research, or anecdotal stories from people's teaching. For every 80 or so pages I read, she had read 10. I figured I must have been a fool this whole time, so the next week I gave the little journals a try. I finished my reading that week in no time. And I also concluded I would never do it again.

The shortened articles seemed like a lot of fluff and not a lot of actual information to make me think. They had too many happy endings, and not enough struggles for my taste. In my experience, very few things just automatically work in a classroom, and nothing works for every student. There are always difficult questions to consider, and often these very short articles didn't take the time to wrestle with those difficult questions. This is not to say that the value of an article is determined by its length. I did read some great articles and interviews which were recommended to me that were only a couple pages long. But reading excerpted pieces simply because they were short turned out to be a fruitless shortcut.

LESSON 3: DON'T TRY TO PROVE SOMETHING; RATHER, SEEK SOURCES THAT MAKE YOU THINK ABOUT SOMETHING

Maybe this seems like a small difference, but for me but it was monumental. I could have sought only articles that argued or helped make some point about how peer critique (the subject of my action research) is great or miserable, but that would have kept me from the great books and articles I read. Some were about motivation and power dynamics or about the history of educational thought. One great article was about how little kids talk with their parents compared to their friends. Because I was just trying to think about teaching, I felt freed up to read articles that didn't seem to relate to my topic. This in turn allowed, or possibly forced, my action research to take twists, turns, and directions that I never intended. This allowed me to move further from my old teaching habits and open up to new discoveries. For example, many of the articles I looked at that were related to my topic talked about power dynamics between teachers and students. I did not want to look at that. It didn't interest me, and it was certainly not the direction I wanted to follow for a year. But the more I read, the more I was forced to think, and the more I realized I was putting my head in the sand by not thinking about power dynamics. Ultimately, being forced to think more deeply about power dynamics is what has changed my classroom the most.

In order to keep myself thinking instead of trying to prove something, I kept my notes minimal while reading articles. It was simply me, a super long article, and a pink highlighter. If something made me think, I highlighted it. After reading a good-sized collection of articles, all those thoughts began to form into a web or jigsaw puzzle of sorts that then allowed me to start designing my own research. I just had to go back and read over my highlights to find where the pieces originally came from.

LESSON 4: LEARN TO EMBRACE BEING OVERWHELMED AND STOP CRAVING A KNOWN ENDING TO YOUR WORK

I was an English major in college, and I'm comfortable with writing without a whole lot of hang-ups or freak-outs. But conceptualizing and writing the lit review section of my research project was something out of my ballpark. In my previous work, I had been able to conceptualize how the end product would read and the overall message I wanted to send. Even if I didn't know what exactly I would write, I always had a planned direction. This was different.

The lit review was so overwhelming I didn't even know where to start. At the point when I needed to start synthesizing information and forming a cohesive draft, I felt like I had read all of these disparate articles, and I didn't know where it was all going. All I could think was, how can I outline hodgepodge? I had no answer, so I didn't try.

My alternate method was much more organic. For each article I simply highlighted things that struck me or seemed interesting to me, even if they didn't obviously relate to my work. After reading an article or two, I did a quick 10- or 15-minute stream of consciousness writing, starting with a quote from one of the articles. I didn't force myself to write about the article; I just wrote about thoughts the article sparked. I think in stories, and often the write-up was about some personal story or memory. As I wrote, I did not think about the larger lit review I would at some point have to write. It was so overwhelming that it just made me freeze up.

When it came time to start writing a synthesized lit review section, I reread my quick writes and did a lot of cutting and pasting. Instead of worrying about an argument or a cohesive work, I treated the synthesis like a larger stream-of-consciousness writing. While this haphazard method went against everything I had ever been taught about "good" writing, I felt I was dealing not with a piece of writing, but with a living beast. It could not be tamed!

When I wrote about a thought that originated in an article I had read, I would write something like, "I think the so-and-so article has a quote about this," or "Add that stuff about that study in New York." By not focusing on the specific quotes, I was able to create a work that had my thoughts in it, instead of a regurgitation of others' studies. I was also able to keep thinking without sifting through hundreds of pages of reading. I went back and did that later. What I ended up with was a solid framework of thoughts to which I would keep adding later.

LESSON 5: THE LITERATURE REVIEW IS A LIVING BEAST AND SHOULD BE TREATED AS SUCH

I know that sounds crazy, but I had never written something that quite honestly seemed alive. At the point when I had written my solid framework, I had only read maybe half of my articles. I kept reading, and more importantly, listening for things people said that sparked thoughts, throughout both the time I was designing my action research and later while I was doing my action research. The lit review and action research definitely overlapped. After I read another article, I would still quick write. But if the article sparked something in me that reminded me of my work, I would also reread my super-rough lit review and see where I might fit it in. Sometimes I would throw it into an already made section. Other times I would just make a new one. If I didn't know where the new section went, I would just tack it onto the end.

LESSON 6: THE FRESH EYES OF FRIENDS AND MENTORS CAN HELP YOU SEE WHAT YOU DIDN'T EVEN KNOW YOU KNEW

Part of writing something that is so untameably beastly is the reality that at some point you need to bring order to it. After I had made my super rough framework, and I had gone back to my articles and added correct quotes and citations, I still had to find a way to make my mishmash of thoughts make sense to others. For most of my work, I could see a progression of thought and rearrange and revise as necessary. I also added subtitles to help me and others follow the order. But there were several significant times when I had added sections although I did not know where they fit, or even if they should be included. At these points I asked a mentor or a friend to read my work. The two people who most often received this honor were my advising professor and a colleague in the same master's program with whom I met every couple of weeks in a coffee shop to trade work. Every time, the person reading my work understood what I wrote, and why I wrote it, more than I did. He or she would usually make a suggestion like "It seems like this should go here," or "It seems like you are trying to say this," and it would all come together. I was often just too immersed in the writing to see it clearly.

LESSON 7: AT SOME POINT, YOU JUST HAVE TO LET THE WILD BEAST GO

When I have spoken to others who are engaged in their action research, they often ask, "How do I know when it is done?" That brings me to the scary part about writing something that is a living beast: It could go on forever. Nearly 3 years later, I still read books, or hear things on TV, or hear teachers talking, and think about my lit review. I could keep adding and writing, but at some point, enough is enough. Eventually, I just felt like it was time to move on and do the action part of my action research, and when I did stumble across problems, I felt like I had already read about possible answers.

LESSON 8: FIND WAYS TO COMPENSATE FOR YOUR OWN IDIOSYNCRASIES

I cannot think of any greater obstacle to my work than my own idiosyncrasies. As previously mentioned, I really dislike sitting, and doing research seems to be the ultimate sitting activity. While I couldn't change my nature, I did find ways to change the work of researching to fit my personality.

My teacher partner had an old exercise bike he never actually used, so I took the handlebars off and built a table that went over it. The table fit my laptop, a bunch of papers, and a glass of wine. I parked the whole monstrosity in my backyard, overlooking the hibiscus and hummingbirds. It made the "sitting" of reading and writing just a little less painful. During the summer, when I had more time, I even packed up my binder of articles and pink highlighter and went camping. I read much of my research by headlamp in Sasquatch country. Under those circumstances, even I might have to admit that research can be enjoyable. The bike table's usefulness lives on, too. I now use it to grade papers, and I am even writing at it right now.

CHAPTER NINE

Emergent Research

Building the Plane While Flying It

BRYAN MEYER

I started my graduate program in education ready to do "real" scientific research. I was interested in collecting "hard," objective data that would provide unambiguous results about how students experienced math in my high school classroom. I toiled over crafting the perfect research question and laying out a structured research methodology, all in the hopes that such foresight would lead me to the truth of my inquiry. The modern scientific research agenda is based on the idea of the neutral observer. By removing ourselves and our subjective experience, it is believed, we can come to know the truths of our world. Furthermore, it is believed that these truths have the potential for societal progress and improvement in the domain of study. Despite my "scientific" beginnings, my research and state of mind evolved over the course of my experience and led me to think quite differently about my own research.

HOW DOES RESEARCH START?

The months leading up to the "beginning" of my action research project were filled with excitement, but also with a pensive sense of probing and reflection. What was it that I was *really* curious about? How would that drive my inquiry? Where would I start? For me it all came back to an experience I had in the first few days of my first year teaching. I remember giving my students the following problem:

> In the NFL, you score 7 points for a touchdown and 3 points for a field goal. If no other opportunities for scoring points are available, which final team scores are possible (for example, is it possible for a team to end the game with 13 points? 14 points?)?

I was expecting curiosity, collaboration, and logical arguments. Instead, I was met with lots of blank stares and students who, seemingly distrusting of their own ability to think and act, were waiting for me to explain the problem away.

At the time, I suppose I didn't know exactly why that was important to me; all I knew was that it *was* important to me. I kept journaling, thinking, and reflecting about similar moments in my classroom that stood out to me. I drafted potential research questions, crossed them out, drafted new questions, crossed those out, and kept refining. I didn't realize it, but I was doing research. It's difficult to say when research really "begins." It's almost as if the process is woven in and through our continuous experience, and its beginning is only somehow approximated in retrospect. Despite the fact that it somehow snuck its way into my experience, all of the questioning, thinking, and reflecting was helpful in beginning to give shape to my more formal inquiry. Words like *authority, agency, problem solving,* and *habits of mind* had started to crop up over and over again in the drafts of my research questions, giving me a vague sense of what I was after. Based on that, I wrote a research question that I thought could guide my inquiry: "How does a classroom centered in mathematical habits of mind foster mathematical agency?" I wanted students to trust their own thinking, I wanted to know what had caused them to lose that trust, and I wanted to know what classroom practices might support the development of intellectual autonomy as a long-range goal of education.

This allowed me to craft a survey that I gave students at the beginning of the year (and the same one again at the end). I asked them to rate their agreement with each statement on a sliding scale (strongly agree to strongly disagree). Some of the statements I provided were:

> I need to learn the steps for how to do a math problem before I can try it on my own.
> It is important to memorize things in mathematics.
> I can create mathematical ideas, formulas, and rules.
> I know how to effectively collaborate with others in making sense of problems.
> I know how to work systematically.

In the end, student responses to some of these statements turned out to be extremely helpful and revealing, while others turned out not to be helpful at all. Mostly, I found the student responses startling and extremely interesting. For instance, I learned that 80% of my students felt they needed to learn the steps for a math problem before they could even begin to try it on their own! To me, this was an early clue about the "hidden curriculum" in many math classrooms; students had learned that, when it comes to mathematics, they need to be told how to think. Of course, this is problematic based on theories of learning, philosophy of mathematics, and epistemology. Most importantly, my survey revealed some important aspects of my students' beliefs and expectations. Rather than trying to control variables and provide baseline data for scientific proof, my survey was a thread woven into my own process of inquiry. Things were off and running, even though I never officially heard the starting gun.

THE EMERGENT MEANING OF *AGENCY*

My action research project came to be centered around what I called "mathematical agency." I wanted to understand how students experienced mathematics classrooms. In retrospect, I can now say that I was curious about what would cause students to act, or not, in the face of novel and unfamiliar mathematical situations. Yet, at the beginning of my research, the word *agency* did not have the same meaning to me as it does now. Rather, drawing from a few distinct classroom experiences and my casual encounters with the word in reading, it had only a shadowy form of the meaning that I would come to assign to it.

That path was not simplistic. I began with a sense of what agency was, based on everything I had read and experienced previously. Yet, I did not "find out" or "confirm" what agency meant through the course of my research. Instead, I *constructed* a meaning from my own experiences with the research. I began to recognize agency (or a lack thereof) when I saw it in action. Paradoxically, it was through recognizing these moments that I began to construct a true sense of what agency was. Essentially, the data helped me to define the very construct I was looking for data about. Each moment helped me refine my own understanding of agency, and in turn, sharpened my focus for future observations and data collection. Consequently, the meaning of *agency* and the aim of my research was a kind of moving target, co-emergent with the inquiry itself.

Traditional scientific research aims to "fix" variables and moving parts in the name of proof and objectivity. That notion is upset when we take a different epistemological stance and realize that the constructs we study, and even the observer him/herself, is changing through the process of observing and researching. There is no stable ground, no way to "fix" our experience or viewpoint. I think it allows us to live *in* our research, move with it, and free ourselves from trying to construct proofs about "the way things are."

Although this may seem ambiguous, I think it is consistent with theories on learning and meaning-making. Humans make meaning from, not prior to, experience. With that in mind, perhaps it becomes necessary to embrace the trepidation and uncertainty that accompanies the early research agenda. It is only through researching that the agenda itself can begin to take form.

RESPONSIVE METHODS

At the beginning of my research, I spent a lot of time thinking and rethinking about how to structure a coherent research methodology. I had pre- and post-surveys, a strict focus group procedure with predetermined interview questions, and a systematic approach to collecting student work samples with the intent to highlight a specific notion of "progress" in their work. These methods, set with an agenda to document progress, proved to be much too rigid. Through the course of my research, much of this structure was dissolved as I became highly responsive to what I was noticing in the classroom and as the path of my own inquiry was laid down in walking. My work became grounded in trying to understand different perspectives and unearthing, rather than minimizing, complexity. It was liberating to think of research as a genuine inquiry.

While I still employed many of the research "tools," the way I engaged with them was radically different than I had anticipated. The questions I asked were determined through my inquiry rather than predetermined prior to it. Much of my research methodology was based in qualitative observational data that was later supplemented and cross-referenced with quantified survey responses. For example, early in the school year there was a moment with one of my students that really stood out to me. While working on an open, exploratory math problem, this student was very resistant, almost refusing to explore because he was convinced the formula he knew "solved" the problem (which it didn't). Stemming from that critical observation, I interviewed the student, conducted a random focus group with similar questions, collected whole class journal answers about the role of the teacher and role of the student, and supplemented all that data with quantified responses from relevant questions from my beginning-of-year survey.

My research methods really began to take shape *with* my actual research. While it is important to have a framework for research methodology going in, I think it is equally important to flex with whatever the enacted research necessitates. I recorded important moments that stood out to me, which I would later call "critical observations." Often, when I would recognize a critical observation, I would organize a demographically heterogeneous focus group to ask deeper questions. A good example was with two of my 12th grade students. They had been working together fabulously one day, eager, energetic, and collaborative, and the very next day (with a new task) seemed dejected and unsure of themselves. I interviewed both of them in addition to hosting a random focus group about what I saw that day; it turned out to be one of the most revealing moments of my research.

In essence, as my inquiry evolved and co-emerged with my findings, it began to necessitate certain research methods. Again, my methods drove research that, in turn, drove the need for evolving methods.

RESEARCHER AS PARTICIPANT AND OBSERVER

Modern science is predicated on the notion of the neutral observer. This idea is disrupted by action research, in which the researcher has an active role in shaping the very environment that the research takes place in. However, even the traditional researcher should be cautious about making claims about "the way things are." The idea of the neutral observer rests on an epistemological premise that our own knowing is somehow a mirror of the world itself. I think of it rather differently. The researcher is implicated in the process of reporting through what they see and what they don't see, in the theoretical framework that they bring to their observations, and in constructing a network of relationships that constitutes their findings. This necessitates actually foregrounding the role of the observer rather than pretending we are able to achieve neutrality by somehow stepping out of our own experience to make an omniscient observation.

All of this might sound rather relativistic. It might sound like a "free pass" for the researcher to do, say, and conclude anything they might desire, as long as they acknowledge their own bias. I disagree. I think it begs the researcher to be a scientist, but a new kind of scientist, one who recognizes that they are defining their inquiry while their inquiry is also defining them. It's much like reading a book more than once. Having been changed by our first reading, we now "find" a new meaning in rereading. The book's meaning will always be of our own making, but the act of reading has changed us and, therefore, changed what we might make of those very same words the next time we read them. Similarly, the researcher will always be moving and changing with/in their research. As I have tried to suggest above, I defined my inquiry, which narrowed my own domain of distinctions and framed my "looking." Yet, I continued to shift, learn, and change as a result of that inquiry, which in turn changed the way I would frame my future inquiries and interpret my past observations. There was no stable world, no firm conclusions that I was uncovering.

This might sound unnatural because of the Western tradition of scientific objectivity that we have been raised in. I find it comforting. To me, it acknowledges all experience as situated in our process of living, and allows us to view research in the same way. Rather than suspending our personal experience for the sake of neutrality, we recognize the inevitability of living, shifting, and becoming through the process of researching. When we recognize the co-emergence of research and researcher, we allow our own presuppositions to break down and make way for new opportunities. It allows the researcher to listen closely to what their participants are saying and to always be looking with open eyes, rather than with ones focused on expected outcomes. It allows the researcher to live in and through their own research, and to recognize that it was never meant to reveal the truth of their inquiry. Instead, as Humberto Maturana and Francisco Varela write in *The Tree of Knowledge*, it is meant to be a "bringing forth of a world through the process of living itself" (1987, p. 11).

WORKS CITED

Maturana, H. R., & Varela, F. J. (1987). *The tree of knowledge: The biological roots of human understanding*. Boston, MA: Shambhala Publications.

CHAPTER TEN

Making Time for Action Research

BERNICE ALOTA

WHO HAS TIME FOR ACTION RESEARCH?

I taught for 8 years before pursuing my graduate degree and being introduced to the idea of "action research." When my graduate program instructors first began discussions around AR, I was intrigued by the idea of acting as a researcher in conjunction with being a teacher, but perplexed as to how I would be able to do both in a thorough, meaningful, and effective way. As a teacher, there were many days when I felt I was barely keeping my head above water—how could I possibly add needs assessments, data collection, data analysis, and reflection into my day? Who has time to reflect?

Little did I know that not only was it possible, but acting as a teacher researcher would enable me to more deeply understand the actions I was taking as an educator in the classroom and to develop ways in which I could improve those actions.

OBSERVATIONS: A STARTING PLACE

My action research took place in a 2nd grade classroom. I had joined this classroom as a teacher in the middle of the second semester and noticed immediately that this group of students was energetic, talkative, enthusiastic, and highly motivated. After knowing me for only a couple of days, students were telling me stories about their home lives, families, interests, and desires. I loved listening to their stories because they were always filled with great detail, excitement, and joy. These students displayed similar enthusiasm for reading, math, science, and geography lessons, and constantly shared everything they knew, or thought they knew, during group discussions.

However, as soon as these same students were given a journal topic or open-ended reader-response question to write about, the excitement seemed to quickly disappear from their eyes, and the first question they asked was always, "How long does my answer have to be?" After several minutes of most of the students staring at a blank page, I then heard, "I don't know what to write." Ten more minutes might pass before students turned in their papers with two to three simple sentences that may or may not have related to each other or the topic at hand.

Before action research, I probably would have dismissed my students' lack of enthusiasm towards writing to "typical 2nd grade behavior" and plugged along with the school's writing program because ... well ... because that was the school's writing program, and with so many responsibilities in the classroom, it's hard to find the time or space to question expectations. However, as a teacher researcher, I forced myself to pause and pushed myself to ask questions.

I wondered—why? Why did a classroom full of energetic, talkative students seem to shut down when it came to writing? Why did students who generally showed excitement for lessons show dread when starting a journal entry? In asking these questions, not only did I focus on observed student behavior and its causes, but for the first time in my teaching career, I made a conscious effort to look internally and think about how I could modify my actions, lessons, planned activities, and the environment I prepared to better serve my students.

NEEDS ASSESSMENT: DIGGING DEEPER

Knowing that changes to my writing program would require time both in and outside of the classroom, it was important to me to engage in a thoughtful needs assessment before getting started. I wanted to ensure that I was heading down the right track by systematically collecting data that would provide me with evidence of and insight into students' attitudes towards writing and the quality of their writing pieces. As a teacher researcher, I felt this data would help me pinpoint how students responded to certain instructional methods and practices. I hoped that it would give me a starting point as to which areas of the writing program needed to be altered, improved, or removed altogether.

Of course, the data collection process itself risked taking time away from teaching and learning, so in choosing my needs assessment design, I identified three data collection approaches that would fit into our normal classroom routines and yield the information and insights I needed—(1) direct student feedback, (2) systematic observation, and (3) analysis of student writing samples.

Direct Student Feedback

Typically, our classroom's writing period lasted 50–60 minutes. However, regardless of the writing prompt or activity, students consistently "finished" their writing assignments approximately 10–15 minutes before the period was over. I decided that during part of that downtime, students could respond to a few questions regarding their general attitude towards that day's writing period, successes they experienced and challenges they met. These questions, or "exit slips," included "What do think went well today?", "What was hard for you today?", and "On a scale of 1–5, how excited were you about this writing activity?" This direct feedback was quick, took advantage of underutilized classroom time, and gave me insight into students' attitudes towards writing, towards themselves as writers, and towards the lesson.

Systematic Observation

During and after writing periods, I also kept an observation journal which focused on student engagement, on- and off-task behavior, questions asked, and other student actions. These observations were different from casual observations that are part of every teacher's day-to-day experience because I focused on students' responses and behaviors specifically related to their writing pieces and their attitudes towards writing. When observing on- and off-task behavior, I counted the number of students off task at regular timed intervals to get a baseline of student engagement and motivation during writing periods. I also took note of what types of activities students were participating in when they were engaged in their writing. Observation notes that I took during class were often shorthand, so it was important that I reviewed my notes every evening while the day's events were still fresh in my memory. This practice took only a few extra moments each evening, and allowed me to identify themes and trends within these notes and to get a general feeling for which part of the period students were most engaged in, which activities students felt most confident participating in, and the areas of writing students had the most challenges with.

Analysis of Student Writing Samples

Finally, I analyzed students' previous writing samples to get a feel for where they were in terms of writing conventions, clarity, and ability to transfer their ideas into their writing. When reviewing their work for purposes of my AR, I wasn't looking for whether or not they followed directions or the rubric; this wasn't about grading the work a second time. Instead, I was comparing the quality of their written work to other finished pieces of work in various subjects to see if there were disparities. I also paid close attention to whether or not their written pieces contained the same uniqueness, enthusiasm, and joy that their verbal stories held. I wanted to determine whether or not students' written pieces were representative of their best work. Because I was already familiar with their work and had previously made comments for student feedback, the analysis process didn't take much time. However, reviewing their writing samples with a specific focus in mind provided me with important understandings about their learning and achievement that I had missed during the routine grading process.

The data I gathered was relatively simple and efficiently fit into my work as a classroom teacher. It also gave me significant insight into my students' feelings towards writing, their current levels of writing proficiency, and their confidence levels regarding writing. Close analysis of student work and my teacher observations revealed that while my students were given focused lessons on writing conventions, spelling, and vocabulary, very few of them applied these lessons to their writing pieces. Furthermore, the evidence I gathered suggested that a majority of my students had difficulty with writing coherently about a specific topic and aimed for the minimum requirements when asked to complete a writing assignment. Finally, after reviewing the exit slips that the students completed, I noticed that most of them expressed a negative attitude towards writing; disliked the process of correcting, editing, and revising; and did not view themselves as capable writers. These insights proved essential in allowing me to craft a meaningful action plan that responded to students' strengths, interests, and needs and fit within the time and context demands of the classroom.

TAKING ACTION: MAKING TIME FOR CLASSROOM RESEARCH

The knowledge I gained about my students during my needs assessment, combined with a review of relevant research literature and conversations with colleagues and advisors, informed my plans to take action in the classroom. Again, here, I worried about how to fit it all in. The day was already packed with activities. How would I find time to accommodate action research? Where would it fit into the school day? What I learned as I began to craft my action plan was that it wasn't about adding more activities, lessons, or plans to the day; it was about approaching the plans with a different lens.

Planning as a teacher researcher was different from the way I typically planned lessons and learning activities. Before action research, I planned lessons based on grade-level standards, time allotted, resources available, and past successes. Student voice played very little part in this equation. However, as a teacher researcher, my action plan was developed in direct response to students' interests, needs, and unique personalities. I continued to utilize student feedback, systematic observation, and close analysis of student work as data collection tools throughout the project; these tools helped me understand what worked, what didn't, and how I could make changes to continue to improve. While this research-oriented process took considerably more effort than my previous lesson-planning approach, it proved to be more effective in fostering an environment where deep learning was taking place—both for the student and the teacher. An action plan developed in direct response to students' strengths and struggles allowed me to optimize class time with my students and allowed them to joyfully create beautiful work.

Action research didn't always fit seamlessly into my life. It did require additional thought, some added time, and a shift in my focus from teacher to teacher researcher. But in the end, the investment proved worthwhile—my students' writing improved dramatically, and they began to see themselves as capable writers and to value the writing process. Moreover, my sense of fulfillment as a teacher and learner grew exponentially, and I now believe wholeheartedly that action research should not be just an added activity in an educator's classroom should time allow. Instead, action research should be an integral part of all teachers' practices in order to perfect their craft and serve their students in the best possible way.

TIPS FOR MAKING TIME FOR AR IN YOUR CLASSROOM

Simple data collection tools can be powerful. Action research does not require complicated charts, graphs, surveys, or activities. Teacher researchers can learn a significant amount about the learning occurring in their classroom through simple means such as purposeful observations and quick writes. These data collection tools are effective and efficient and can fit seamlessly into any classroom with minimal planning and preparation.

Look for existing practices and work samples that can be used for a new purpose. Teacher researchers can use existing classroom activities and student work as a way to assess the needs of their students in regards to action research. With AR, many times it is not about doing more things, but about doing and seeing certain things in a different way.

Take the first step and don't be afraid to "fail." In all areas in life, failure is the ultimate teacher. Don't waste time thinking that you can't get started until everything is perfect. Don't be afraid to take action for fear it won't work. Don't be paralyzed by the fear that you might do something wrong. Jump in! Missteps, challenges, and incorrect assumptions will teach you invaluable lessons, and they may even lead you to exciting discoveries through doors you never even knew existed.

CHAPTER ELEVEN

Data Collection

How My Research Methods Became My Greatest Assessment Tools

SARAH STRONG

I have always had ideals for what my classroom should look and sound like, and perhaps even larger ideals for what students should think and feel about the math they are working on. The problem was, I hadn't really ever asked them what they were feeling, so I didn't know if my ideals were becoming reality. As I began designing my methods for my action research project about how students experienced open-ended math problems, I knew that I needed to figure out what the students were feeling. But this was math class. Would students want to share their feelings? Would students be honest? Would students be thoughtful and reflective?

These questions hung in the air as I distributed journals on the first day of class and passed out writing prompts to paste on the front covers. These writing prompts had questions like "How did this problem make you *feel*?" That very day, we began work on our first open-ended math problem together in class. I purposefully wrapped up class 5 minutes early so we could have time to write in journals. The moment of truth came—the moment when the students would either stand up and boycott writing about their feelings in math class, or sit down and do it (in all honesty, I was expecting the former). Much to my surprise, the students silently and diligently wrote in their journals, sometimes filling up more than one page and often expressing more depth of thought than I had imagined them capable of! Their writing that day elaborated on their thinking and gave me a deeper look at their math written on the opposite pages. Flipping through their journals, I felt like I had hit the jackpot!

This feeling continued throughout my research. In their journals, some students expressed excitement about their math work and eloquently discussed their feelings while solving problems:

> When I read this problem, I was excited because I could feel my wheels turning! Now I am not afraid to mess up, but I can try new things. I've got to be like a detective looking for new patterns!

With the words of this student, I was able to see how he looked at the problem: like a detective looking for clues. Having this problem-solving strategy in 6th grade language helped me to articulate supports for other struggling students. I was even able to create a "Tips for Students by Students" section on the resource page of my final action research report, as a result of the comments from students' journals.

Another student commented:

> I was surprised that the math problem was just my level and that I was able to finish it before people put down the answer on the board. I was nervous about not being able to figure it out. I was happy about figuring out a pattern for the answer.

By expressing her surprise, nervousness, and happiness, this student helped me to understand that the key for students is having a problem that is right at their level. It also helped me to see that nerves are a large part of the battle, and that I needed to address this as we took on future problems.

Other students expressed frustration and distaste for the problem:

> No, I didn't like this problem one bit. There were too many things to do and it was confusing.

> This problem was hard for me 'cause I didn't see the pattern till shortly later and I had no clue how to use it.

Responses like this helped me to better support students on an individual level and to gain a deeper insight for why students would sometimes shut down when a problem was presented to them.

The students' math work now had a narrative, and so also did my journey as a math teacher. Their words helped to guide me in what to teach and follow up on the next day, and also how to provide extra supports to students who were expressing confusion or frustration. I found that something as simple as a math journal would become the most important type of assessment in my classroom because it helped me understand students' mathematical thinking, but also the feelings behind their thinking.

DATA COLLECTION METHODS TO GET IN STUDENTS' HEADS

As it turned out, student journals were not the only treasure trove of information about my students and their feelings. As I tackled more of my data collection methods, like interviews, quick understanding checks, and surveys, I was further enlightened as to how quickly the methods I had set out to use were becoming more than just a means for collecting data for a research study.

Journals

During my action research, math journals became and still are for me the most important piece of formative assessment in my classroom. When I designed the journals, I was thinking of them purely as a way of gathering data. Throughout the year, however, the journals became the driving force in my instruction. Each open-ended problem that the students engaged in was done in a specific math journal that was organized at the beginning of the school year.

In the front of the journal, students had both a table of contents and a list of reflection questions. Some days they would answer all the questions, and others I would select two of them to reflect on. These questions (with accompanying sentence starters) were as follows:

1. How did you feel when you initially read this problem?
   - I was surprised that ...
   - I was nervous about ...
   - I was happy about ...
2. What did you learn from this problem?
   - Some math I learned was ...
   - Some strategies I learned were ...
   - Next time I would like to ...
3. What are some tips you would give a friend about this problem?
   - First you should ...
   - Don't worry about ...
   - In order to solve this problem quickly you could ...
   - Here are four quick steps for solving this problem.
4. Overall, did you like this problem?
   - This problem was hard/easy/medium because ...
   - I would/would not recommend Mrs. Strong use this problem again because ...

I collected and reviewed their journals after each problem, not only to grade them, but also to look at their various strategies and extract quotes from their reflections. Having all of their open-ended problems condensed in one journal provided me with a quick way to flip through their work seeking trends and notable exceptions, both of which were informative to my research. As I read through journals, I would record notable quotes and thoughtful statements that stood out to me. Each problem had a spreadsheet of quotes associated with it, and each quote was coded with a student number (which they had labeled on their journals at the beginning of the year). The process of using this spreadsheet to collect quotes helped me to quickly sift through data at the end, seeking trends and words that came up often. Recording quotes was rather quick and easy, and I became accustomed to doing this while I graded. For a more in-depth look at students' thinking in journals, I carefully selected six focus students who represented the spectrum of my class in terms of sex, race, and academic performance on our preassessment at the beginning of the year. These were also the students that I ended up interviewing, so focusing in on their journals gave me a foundation with which to look at the larger journal data.

Another benefit of these journals was that they guided me in deciding which problems I should use in the coming years, which I should change, and which missed the mark completely. Students would make comments like, "I would recommend Mrs. Strong use this problem again because it really makes you think, no matter how smart you are," or "I would recommend not putting the sub questions with an x, xi, xii … because it puts too much pressure on me when I have more than one problem to solve and explain." These comments helped me to edit and refine the problems for future use. The use of student journals as a means of formative assessment was integral in my research, and has since been integral in my development as a teacher in the years following my research.

Interviews

As I learned about methods of data collection, I set my mind on doing interviews. What better way to get into students' heads, I thought, than to talk to them in the quiet of my office? However, the first few interviews felt dry and contrived. It felt like the students were just telling me what I wanted to hear (something along the lines of, "Oh, yes, Mrs. Strong, I absolutely LOVE these math problems, they are making me a better person every day!"). For the grade level I was working with, 6th grade, the desire to please is still quite central to their conversations with me at school. This played out in our interviews and, although it felt nice on a superficial level, it was not particularly constructive for my research. Other tools like the aforementioned journals, quick understanding checks, surveys, and my own internal monologue ended up becoming invaluable tools that continue to be a part of my assessment practice today.

Quick Understanding Checks

Another method that worked wonders for me was quick understanding checks at the end of a period. I usually only took 1 minute to do this, but the act of a quick check-in helped me streamline my assessment efforts and gain lots of useful data.

These understanding checks were as simple as a blind survey where the students put their heads down and held up a number to rate the difficulty of an assignment on a scale. In one instance I asked the students to "rate their confusion level on a scale of 1 to 5 … one being most confused." When I saw lots of 1s pop up, I knew that I needed to provide extra scaffolds for the following day and tackle the problem in a different way. There was one time that the responses I got caused me to completely abandon a problem and move onto something different. I learned that if my students weren't engaged because the level of the content was too high or too low for them, it was not worthy of our classroom time. Another form of these check-ins was an exit slip with one problem designed to identify misconceptions in the day's activities. On one occasion I asked them to put away all their work and simply "restate" what they were working on in the problem. It was amazing to see that after a day's work, there were students who were unclear on their purpose. This insight enabled me to properly scaffold the next day's activities and pointed me in the direction of individual students I needed to check in with.

Surveys

Surveys were an important part of my data collection because they provided quantifiable and comparable data from students. Of even more importance was giving the same survey at a few points during the year, because I was able to track student responses quickly and easily. I created and administered a survey to each of my 56 students to gather quantitative data and seek trends in their general feelings about math and ideas about various types of math problems. The same survey was given at the beginning, middle, and end of my study, to seek changes in students' feelings about these types of problems as the semester progressed. One of the questions on the survey was:

How would you describe yourself as a math student?

a) I'm a math genius … give me any problem and I'll solve it for you.
b) I'm pretty good at math … it's my best subject.
c) Math is alright … I am improving at it.
d) I don't think I'm good at math at all.
e) Other ________________

As you can see, I tried to word the question in language that was familiar to my students (in this case, I aimed the phrasing at a 6th grade audience).

Furthermore, having this baseline data about the students' feelings allowed me to cross-reference this with their documented feelings on future problems, essentially triangulating across data sources. For example, it is not very noteworthy if a student who considers him-/herself to be a math genius performed well on a given problem. On the contrary, a student who doesn't think they are very good at math saying that they enjoyed a given problem would be high praise, and cause to think that the problem was a "good" problem. In my study, I created a scatterplot comparing students' experiences on open-ended problems to their preassessment score at the beginning of the year. The graphed data showed that students with scores from 10 all the way up to 39 on the preassessment (out of 40 points total) reported positive experiences on the problems. The three students who reported negative experiences had scores of 18, 33, and 36. This data provided hard evidence that these problems could work for all kids, not just the high or low achievers. Similarly, the few students for whom they weren't working represented the whole spectrum as well. Having baseline data from surveys like the one above is an excellent way to paint a starting picture of your students, and can provide a great foundation to show progress of feelings and thought throughout the year.

Observations and My Own Internal Dialogue

Though it wasn't in my official "methods" section of my research, I realized that my informal observations of students' needs and how I responded to those needs played a large role in students' work on open-ended problems. Below is a list of questions that I regularly ask myself and want to continue to ask myself in my coming years of teaching:

- What needs are my students bringing to the classroom today that might impact their learning, and how can I help take care of these needs?
- Are any students sitting around with nothing to do because they finished early?
- Are any students so confused that they don't know where to start?
- Do the students seem excited about what they are working on?
- Are the students talking to one another about their work?
- Are students talking to me about their work?

By daily gauging my students' feelings and experiences with the above questions through informal observation, I have learned to tailor my activities, sometimes even changing plans in the middle of a lesson to make sure that I am meeting all of the students' needs. It also helps to remind me that my students are people coming to class with their own sets of baggage, just as I am. To disregard this "baggage" would be a failed opportunity to reach out to a student in need, and a failed learning opportunity.

***

As a researcher, my classroom is my laboratory. I seek out trends and outliers and try to make sense of my data, using this data to better my practice day by day. In the design phase of the action research, I strategically selected data collection and analysis methods to elicit the simplest and most useful information daily while in my "laboratory." As I used my instruments, I came to see trends that were useful for my research, and that also became a useful means of consistent formative assessment in my classroom. This formative assessment is not only content-based, but also based on self-efficacy and the notion that students will respond and learn better when they feel safe, cared for, and listened to.

CHAPTER TWELVE

The Stories AT THE Heart OF Our Research

CADY STAFF

I have always loved stories. I love reading and writing them, and most of all, I love helping students find their own. Great stories can be found all around us. Recently, I read *Don't Let the Pigeon Drive the Bus!* with my 3-year-old niece, and I laughed so hard along with her that tears came streaming down my face. It captures the essence of that defiance and mischievousness that bubbles up in 3-year-olds, and so it touches the 3-year-old in all of us. Great children's stories do a beautiful job of identifying a poignant, silly, joyful, or powerful moment and bringing it to life through words and drawings. That is what I wanted my action research to achieve. I wanted my students' and my shared journey to become a story worth sitting down and reading—alone or aloud—capturing the essence of our moments together. I wanted my thesis to illustrate that the most compelling stories are not always fiction, but rather those that ring most true. Looking back, it is hard to believe that all of those stories came in response to one initial question.

My initial inquiry was "What happens when social entrepreneurship and the new capitalism become an integral part of my classroom curriculum?" (Not exactly the title of the next best-selling children's book. ...) The only way to answer that question, in the end, was through a collection of messy, beautiful, inspiring, and challenging stories. It was in the co-designing of the project, the listening, documenting, writing, and reflecting, that my students and I grew as learners and storytellers. Ultimately, the question and the answers faded into the background of our shared story.

As a kid, my first attempts at storytelling involved filling 25-cent notebooks with stories. I would read those stories aloud to my parents or friends or anyone who would listen. My natural inclination when telling a story is to write it out. My students capture and tell their own stories much differently, these days. They often tell their stories digitally and publicly with mixed media. They post movies and artwork, along with choice words when they feel they will help us see more clearly what they are trying to show us. I wanted my action research to be about my students and to capture the essence of our shared learning journey—our story. I knew our project would not end with me sitting on the floor with my students, opening up my thesis to read aloud as we all laughed and cried together—but it doesn't hurt to dream. I did want my action research to be a co-constructed story of adventure with all of our voices represented authentically, merging the styles of my good ol' pen-and-paper method and their multimedia approach to storytelling. And so my web-page thesis was born. The link became live, and the potential audience grew exponentially.

During the gathering information phase of my action research, I became more of a data hoarder than a gatherer and analyzer. Whenever we were introduced to a new method of gathering evidence or reflections from students, I implemented it the next day or next week in my classroom. A few weeks into the project, I had recorded interviews, compiled journals full of reflections, amassed messy piles of exit slips spewing out of overloaded file folders, captured video footage, e-mailed surveys, and transcribed interviews. I buried myself in data, which was an important step for me (but not one that I would necessarily recommend). As I dug myself out of that first mixture of data methods, I held tight to the ones that provided rich information and helped my students' stories emerge. My three favorite methods of gathering data eventually became: short-response surveys that received an instant response from every student in the class (so that I could use what they told me to co-construct the next steps of our project), interviews (formal and informal, where I could ask my students questions and listen to their answers, and follow up with more questions), and video (which captured every moment as it happened, so that I was recording everything, not just what I was looking for).

FINDING (NOT FORCING) THE STORY

The problem with storytellers like me is that they often identify one story and want to make everything connect and feed into that one story (which has the potential to blind them to other emerging stories). I admit it—I had a story in mind when I started my action research. By having this story in mind, I constructed my first set of questions (a pre-survey) to get to the heart of the story I thought I would find. Luckily, I asked a few questions to check if my story was true before I jumped into telling it. My first quick survey quickly showed me that the story of transformation I was hoping to tell had happened long before our project began.

Originally, I thought I would look closely at how my students defined success before the project began versus after their participation in the Social Entrepreneurship Project. I wanted to write a story about how my students and I developed a newfound passion for changing the world for the better—but the survey responses showed me that we all already had that passion going in. My assumption that my students would have at the start a profit-driven definition of success was a misconception. As I read the well-rounded definitions my students had for their own personal success, I realized that I did not need to focus on broadening those definitions. When asked to define success, students wrote answers like "Success doesn't have to be like rich and stuff, success is more that you have a happy life and loving family." Another student wrote that success means "joy and hard work." After reading their responses, the focus of the project changed. I was no longer setting out to change my students' definitions of success. My original, inauthentic story of students transforming from money-grubbers to world changers was laid to rest. I felt ashamed for underestimating my students, but grateful that a quick full-class survey could enlighten me. After that first survey, my action research became less about constructing one prescribed story of a full-class transformation and more about focusing on the much more complex and varied stories of student engagement, perseverance, and empowerment. I was no longer convincing my students to change the world; I was charged with giving them the tools, encouragement, and support they needed to make that change.

Throughout my action research, I often asked the whole class to fill out similar short surveys that would give me a sense of their feelings, understandings, and progress through the project. Sometimes, these surveys were sent over e-mail and other times they were required as exit slips from class. It was challenging, but worthwhile, to read those surveys the moment they were turned in so that I could respond in a timely manner to what my students were saying. Those surveys that were left in a drawer over the weekend quickly became irrelevant, and a waste of time and paper. My best full-class surveys required short responses that students could provide and I could process efficiently. For example, I could ask every student to respond in two sentences to the question: "What is one challenge and one success you have experienced in your social business group so far?" I knew the heart of my students' stories would not be found in those surveys, but that is where I uncovered clues to the stories that I should pursue further.

CHOOSING THE STORIES: A CASE FOR CASE STUDIES

There is a good reason most stories do not have 56 main characters. At first, I wanted to tell every student's story as we journeyed through the Social Entrepreneurship Project together. They all had hopes, dreams, relevant past experiences, personal connections to causes, and beautiful stories worth capturing and sharing. Yet, it was not possible to do justice to any individual story while trying to tell all of them at once. So, I looked through early surveys to get a sense of common themes of the stories emerging.

Initially, I planned to choose focus students for my research based on their experiences and varied responses to interview questions and reflections. I was hoping that by choosing individual students from as many different groups as possible, I could make the story representative of the whole class. Halfway through the project, I changed my approach, and I chose three groups to focus on as case studies. I was finding such an interesting variety of responses and reflections from within individual groups. The dynamic of these varying degrees of engagement, perseverance, and empowerment from within a group were as intriguing and impactful as the individual stories of each student's experience. After a few group interviews, it became clear that because students were working so closely in their groups, they were not telling different stories; they were providing different perspectives on the same narrative. In the end, I chose three specific groups as my case studies because they represented the three main approaches groups were taking to creating their social businesses. On top of full-class surveys and check-ins, I gathered data from these case study groups using student interviews, reflections, and video footage. The plot thickened.

ALLOWING CASE STUDIES TO TELL THEIR TRUE STORIES

Trying to understand my students' experiences of engagement, perseverance, and empowerment (or the lack thereof, at times) was at the heart of all of the questions I asked them. One question that struck me from video interviews was "What allows some groups to persevere and overcome challenges, while other groups hit roadblocks and cannot seem to get past them?" It was not necessarily that question, but the follow-up questions and the discussion surrounding that question that shined a light on some of the best developing stories. I realized, especially when it came to one of my case studies, that I had misinterpreted their decision to create a polished social business plan as their final product rather than taking small, measurable action. I would have stuck to this misconception if not for a follow-up video interview with the group.

Before the interview, I feared they were giving up, so we talked about that. They explained that their decision was based on a well-thought-out conclusion they had made about social businesses and instruments of social change:

> I think there are a lot of microscopic social businesses kind of mucking up the field. I think that there are so many little ones, if they were all to come together and work for the bigger

> ones ... it's just like a capitalist market. You want the Googles out there, because then they're able to provide a lower cost to make a bigger change.

Their final product of a "microscopic social business" plan was meant to serve as the foundation for other larger, more impactful plans for future student groups. What I had misinterpreted as their giving up on their ability to make social change, at first, was actually an act of perseverance in itself—not settling for a small plan they thought would fizzle, but offering a strong foundation for a larger change they believed would be possible in the future. This group had developed a healthy appreciation for the planning steps of long-term future gains rather than small-scale, short-term gain. They challenged my own misconceptions about what perseverance means for a group of budding social entrepreneurs. They also revealed an interesting story of group dynamics. By allowing my students to answer questions in interviews with follow-up questions instead of a one-dimensional survey, my students were able to explain their thinking and justify their choices. They just needed time and space to tell their story—and I just needed to make the time and space to really listen before making judgments.

I also needed to find ways to let students tell their own stories. One way I did this was by creating a video montage introducing each of the case study groups in my final thesis. The students and I captured footage throughout the project and worked together to create each group's final montage. Most of my richest findings emerged from the video footage I collected and that students shared with me along the way. When I write about that footage, I can capture what I learned from my students, but the raw footage was where the most authentic storytelling took place. And that was my goal—to tell the story of our shared learning journey. I kept watching my students tell their stories so beautifully through video footage, and I tried to do justice to their stories and our shared findings with my words. In the end, I included their videos because I knew we had to tell the story together.

REVISING OUR STORY TOGETHER

I often feel I do not really learn what I have learned until I have written about it and revised it. So, from the very beginning, I tried to write down everything I could about our shared journey through the Social Business Project. I asked my students to capture their experiences regularly with video along the way too. Before my final thesis was posted online, my students shared their video introductions for feedback and final edits, and I shared sections of my thesis with them.

Each time I shared my work and questions with my students, they gave me a fresh perspective. They pointed out misconceptions and celebrated with me when I got it right. Students enjoyed seeing their thoughts and reflections quoted in a thesis next to the expertise of famous researchers. Together, we saw how our shared experiences made us quotable experts on the Social Entrepreneurship Project. One student, who took my thesis home to read it before signing a letter saying he approved of posting the material on the web, said, "It's so cool we're a part of this study. I think this will really catch on." Three years later, 2,982 people (and climbing) have visited my digital thesis to share in our story.

CHAPTER THIRTEEN

What Makes Action Research Good Research?

STEPHEN F. HAMILTON

Many people regard research as a mysterious activity accessible only to a small cadre of impossibly smart and formidably educated people. Those who engage in research understand that it is a disciplined inquiry process, distinctive from everyday learning and problem solving in having explicit standards for what is valid and in making public its methods and results. The first conception is more commonly associated with scientific research. It seems close to reality in some realms of the physical and natural sciences. The second conception fits more readily with the kinds of research done by historians, lawyers, and students writing term papers. But even in the rarefied domains of genomics and astrophysics we should take comfort in reflecting that scientific methods were not devised for the exclusive use of geniuses; indeed, they regularize the process of scientific discovery so that ordinarily smart people can participate.

If action research is closer to everyday thought processes than theoretical physics, what are the criteria for evaluating it? Among the many plausible answers to this question, the key point for me is that good action research gives the researcher (and others) a deeper understanding of and greater control over—meaning, in this context, the capacity to act effectively on—the phenomenon in question. Understanding and control (including manipulation and prediction) are standard criteria for evaluating research, but there are different emphases in research along the basic-applied continuum. The search for the Higgs boson, the "God particle" that is essential to physicists' Standard Model, is clearly about understanding our universe. Its recent discovery by an international team using the Large Hadron Collider at CERN is very important theoretically, but what, if anything, it will allow us to do is far from clear. In contrast, the search for low-cost energy storage, if successful, will make sustainable energy much more feasible, a clear and important case of gaining control over our environment. Though that search relies on fundamental physical principles, as an engineering project it will not likely yield deeper understanding of the principles of physics.

I use the terms *basic* and *applied* reluctantly because they imply a dichotomy. Stokes (1997) has a much more useful typology. For him the key issue is whether research is "inspired by considerations of use" or by the "quest for fundamental understanding" (p. 73). Action research falls into the first category, the search for the Higgs boson into the latter. But he also distinguishes research according to its impact, noting that much research has little or no impact, whether inspired by use or by the quest for understanding. His paragon is Louis Pasteur, whose fundamental discoveries in microbiology resulted from research undertaken to prevent milk from sickening children and to guide the work of brewers and vintners. For Stokes, Pasteur epitomizes "use-inspired basic research," a category that combines basic with applied instead of seeing them as mutually exclusive.

My own research has always been motivated by questions that arise from practice. Researchers who consider their work "basic" usually get their questions from previous research. I think starting with practice is more challenging because when a researcher's questions come from others' research, she or he can build on the theories, methods, and research designs that have already been used rather than having to work out how to conceptualize the problem and how to gather and interpret pertinent data.

CRITERIA FOR EVALUATING ACTION RESEARCH

Action research, by definition, is applied social research. It is much more analogous to engineering than to physics. It is also *local* research. Rather than seeking to discover *universal* laws, as most researchers do who think of themselves as "basic," action researchers aim to act effectively upon a local phenomenon; they hope to change it for the better. This local-universal distinction makes standard criteria about "external validity" and generalizability less important in action research than "authenticity" in its own context (Lincoln & Guba, 2007) and informing effective action.

What Makes a Good Literature Review?

Action researchers want to use their understanding to effect change, something that most "basic" researchers leave to others. Understanding can be pursued directly through new empirical research and indirectly by studying what other researchers have learned and thought about related phenomena. Combining the two is ideal;

that's what the "lit review" is about. Too often undertaken as an obligatory exercise, a good literature review identifies critical insights from theory and from previous empirical research into the question the researcher has posed. As noted above, when the researcher's question comes from practice, the potential sources of insight can seem infinite. An anonymous cynic noted, "The world has problems and universities have departments." The painful truth behind this jibe is that real-world problems rarely fit neatly into academic disciplines. As a result, starting with a practice question opens a vast range of potentially relevant literature.

An action researcher might want to locate her question in demography: How many people are affected and what are their characteristics? History could locate the question in time: Is it old or new? How has it changed over time? Psychology, the most common discipline referenced in education research, might yield insights into relevant studies of motivations, emotions, thoughts (cognition), and social relations. Sociology is more about groups and subgroups of people and their behavior in a social structure. The possibilities really are nearly endless. Trying to touch all the bases will immobilize you!

I recommend beginning with introspection. Whose writing has influenced the way you think about your question? For me, Dewey and Bronfenbrenner are touchstones; I nearly always find myself returning to work by one or both of them when I start a new project. Remind yourself of what those who have influenced you wrote, and think hard about how that applies to your question. Then branch out. Use literature search methods to get outside what is already familiar to you. But avoid making an impossibly long list of sources. Start with what seem the most important and note whom those sources cite. The old-fashioned (pre–Google Scholar) method of following trains of citations is still valuable because you are reading things that influenced influential scholars.

Rather than simply citing selected works, the literature review should be a kind of intellectual biography of the problem, tracing what others have thought and learned that is related to your question and how it has shaped the study you are doing. It's not a once-and-done step. Think of yourself as engaging in a continuous dialog with other scholars as you design your study, collect and analyze data, and then report your results. The discussion or conclusions section of your report should reconnect with the key sources you identified in the literature review, indicating where your findings fit or what they have added to the literature. By linking your local effort to previous research, you are taking it in the direction of the universal and helping others envision how it might apply in their own settings.

Effecting Change

I propose that action research is good when actions undertaken as part of it ultimately yield the anticipated results. That is what I mean by *change* (a better term than *control* in this context). If a teacher conducts action research to understand how to help students with different reading skills work collaboratively, the test of the research is evidence that they are working better collaboratively. *Ultimately* is an important modifier because achieving change will likely take multiple iterations of the cycle Stringer (1996) calls "look, think, act."

This criterion, like other scientific standards, is quite stringent. If the teacher acts on what he thinks he has learned about collaboration and sees no improvement, it may be because his actions were not adequately aligned with his understanding, not because he has misunderstood the phenomenon. Moreover, it is entirely possible to have a very good grasp of what conditions promote collaboration but still be unable to create those conditions. Failure to achieve anticipated results could result from looking for the wrong evidence, or measuring improvement incorrectly. Yet another possibility is that improved collaboration might be demonstrated but attributable to factors the teacher does not fully understand. In sum, linking understanding to subsequent change is not adequate to demonstrate that one has done high quality research, but it helps.

Replicability or Trustworthiness?

Replicability is a key criterion for evaluating research. In the lab sciences, literal replication is common. Outside of laboratories, actual replication is rare. However, replicability is often held up as a principle and then addressed indirectly. If a historian bases claims on archival documents, another historian should, at least in principle, be able to examine the same documents and come up with the same or a similar interpretation. This is not literally replication, but it is an instance of the same principle that the researcher's activities and conclusions are open to checking by another independent researcher. Social scientists evaluate research on the basis of the quality of its design and measures and whether they adequately represent the theoretical framework and justify the conclusions. That is why authors of journal articles are expected to provide sufficient detail so that another researcher could, in principle, replicate the study. Publication is a critical part of research, not only as a way of communicating to others what one has learned but also as a way of opening one's work to criticism.

Replicability is in some ways incompatible with action research, where the researcher is intimately connected to the phenomenon under investigation and the phenomenon is local rather than universal. A more useful term that addresses the same issues is *trustworthiness* (Lincoln & Guba, 1985). One way to think about trustworthiness in action research is to ask, "Why should anyone believe what I think I have learned?" This question can be turned inward and outward. Every researcher should keep in mind at all times the inward version: "How can I be sure I really know what I think I know?" The tough version of the outward question is,

"How can I convince a skeptic that I have found something that is both true and worthwhile?"

Focusing on trustworthiness rather than replicability means setting aside the question of whether what you found would also be found somewhere else, and focusing on how to be confident about what you found. Documenting change is a good place to start. The greater challenge is demonstrating causal links between changes you made in your practice and "outcomes," changes in student performance or behavior. Detail, logic, and conscientious consideration of alternative explanations help to make your account of those links more persuasive. (Logic models are great tools for this purpose. They are better known in the world of youth development and evaluation, but have clear utility in education. See W. K. Kellogg Foundation, 2006; University of Wisconsin, 2010.)

Challenging Your Own Findings and Interpretations

Good research entails continually exposing one's own biases, preconceptions, and emerging understandings to the possibility of disproof. Good research systematically counters the human weakness of confirmation bias: the tendency to attend to, remember, and believe evidence that is consistent with what one already believes and to dismiss inconsistent evidence. Good action research systematically seeks both confirming and disconfirming evidence. It is designed not only to prove a point but to disprove the same point and to disprove alternative or competing points (hypotheses, understandings). Let's say that your question is about how to avoid gender bias in students' participation in projects. You might report that after you made a change in the procedure for allocating tasks to students, the previously observed tendency of boys to choose the manual tasks and girls to do more writing disappeared. Your interpretation that it was this change that made the difference will be more persuasive if you also report that you tried three other changes and they made no difference.

A brief digression on epistemology, the philosophy of knowledge. Inductive reasoning, that is, gathering evidence to support a conclusion, by its nature can never yield absolute proof. If you want to prove that all swans are white you have to observe not only all existing swans but all possible swans. One black swan (the icon of this discussion) disproves your conclusion. This is why hypothesis-testing science is designed to disprove the "null hypothesis." If your hypothesis is that not all swans are white and then you do everything conceivable to find a swan that isn't white and fail, your results are likely to convince most people even though you do not and never will have absolute proof; a black swan might someday turn up. The philosopher Karl Popper (2002/1959) propounded the principle that all scientific claims must be falsifiable, which has the corollary that the scientist's duty is to take all feasible steps to falsify his or her own claims.

Action research that builds in tests of the researcher's conclusions and then communicates the methods and results to others in sufficient detail is more convincing than lawyerly arguments that only include evidence and interpretations supporting the researcher's case. Many of the same activities that promote self-testing also add credibility to nonparticipants. Reporting on the steps one has taken to promote skepticism and to try to prove oneself wrong makes findings more credible to outsiders, including those inclined to skepticism. The role of critical friends is in part to push back against a researcher's assumptions and question premature conclusions. Colleagues who participate in data collection and analysis together not only provide assistance but can double-check an investigator's procedures and conclusions. "Member checks" (Lincoln & Guba, 1985), periodic reviews of tentative findings with students, colleagues, and others who are involved in the phenomenon in question, are another way to test emerging understandings.

Generalizability

Generalizability is essential to universal research. Recognizing that action research is local research, not intended to yield universal truths, one can still push the boundaries of what local means. Are new understandings and resulting capacity to effect change limited to this semester's 2nd-period class, or can they be "replicated" in another class? In several classes? When a colleague learns about the new understandings and takes similar actions, does she get the same results? What about a teacher in a different school?

Posing questions like these and conducting research to investigate them is a way of further deepening understanding. Learning that a colleague achieved the same results but in a somewhat different way may affirm understandings while broadening the definition of what is central. Learning how a new approach worked or did not work in a different school can help clarify what conditions contribute to the phenomenon that the researcher had not initially attended to because they were built into her school.

CONCLUSIONS

The goals of action research and the principles underlying its design have much in common with other forms of research. All research is a process of discovering, an effort to understand something better. Action research is distinctive in being local; it is explicitly about understanding a particular setting, making no claims to uncovering universal truths. In this it is more like ethnography than lab science. It is also unapologetically applied, using deeper understanding to effect change, which is itself a critical test of understanding. Like all good researchers, action researchers incorporate previous theory and findings into their work and systematically try to probe and even disprove their own ideas. Then, when they report what they have learned clearly and compellingly, they can improve their own practice and that of others, and add their contribution to the continuing discourse among scholars.

WORKS CITED

Lincoln, Y. S., & Guba, E. G. (1985). *Naturalistic inquiry*. Beverly Hills, CA: Sage.

Lincoln, Y. S., & Guba, E. G. (2007). But is it rigorous? Trustworthiness and authenticity in naturalistic evaluation. *New Directions for Evaluation, 114*, 15–25.

Popper, K. (2002). *The logic of scientific inquiry* (Classics ed.). New York: Routledge. (First published in English 1959)

Stokes, D. E. (1997). *Pasteur's quadrant: Basic science and technological innovation*. Washington, DC: The Brookings Institution.

Stringer, E. (1996). *Action research: A handbook for practitioners*. Thousand Oaks, CA: Sage.

University of Wisconsin. (2010). *Logic model.* Retrieved from http://www.uwex.edu/ces/pdande/evaluation/evallogicmodel.html

W. K. Kellogg Foundation. (2006). *W. K. Kellogg Foundation logic model development guide*. Retrieved from http://www.wkkf.org/resource-directory/resource/2006/02/wk-kellogg-foundation-logic-model-development-guide

SECTION THREE

Engaging Student Voice

> When I first started my research I wasn't aware how different the students' perception is from my perception. I learned to ask them questions and then listen to them. I just find that to be the most helpful thing, just directly asking them ... That's one huge thing I learned from AR.

This statement, shared by one of the graduates of our teacher education program, echoes the sentiments of many who have gone through action research—a critical element of our learning as teacher researchers comes from learning to listen to our students' voices. This concept seems obvious; after all, as teachers we encounter student voices all day, every day. But learning to step back and really hear what they are saying is, unfortunately, not always a standard part of our teaching practice. This is understandable. We are busy, there are always competing student demands, some student complaints are way off base, and let's face it, sometimes it can be pretty intimidating to ask students for their honest input. But when we slow down and open the conversation to listen to student voices we often learn remarkable things about our students, our teaching, and ourselves.

In my own teaching some of my most powerful learning took place when I listened to the voices of my students. As a brand new high school history teacher I was initially annoyed and somewhat insulted when my students asked the proverbial question "Why do we have to learn this?" I thought that I had selected relevant materials and was making appropriate connections between the past and the present. But when I finally got over my sense of righteous indignation and really listened to my students, I recognized that appropriate connections were not the same as meaningful connections. I needed to do a better job of asking questions and providing learning experiences that would allow students to recognize universal themes and recurring dilemmas from the past and to relate those concepts to their own experiences.

Student voice emerged as an important theme years later when I transitioned from classroom teacher to doctoral student. For my dissertation research I studied the experiences of teachers from six different urban high schools who had been identified as effective by both students and administrators. These teachers differed in many ways, including their own personal and professional backgrounds, years of experience, race and ethnicity, educational backgrounds, and experience in teacher education and professional development. But one element that they all shared was that somewhere along the way they had learned to listen to their students. One teacher, who had had her daughter as one of her students, reflected on the learning that took place when she listened as her own child struggled with the material, "It was like an epiphany ... I really had to look at my teaching. If I wasn't meeting her needs, I knew there were other kids in the class I was missing too. That's where I had my breakthrough."

Research into larger issues of education reform has similarly found that there is tremendous power in asking students to help adults rethink how to improve learning and teaching in schools (Joselowsky, 2005; Yonezawa & Jones, 2009.) In his book on educational change Michael Fullan describes students as "vastly underutilized resources," noting that they often have insights and ideas about ways to strengthen schooling that otherwise might be overlooked by teachers and administrators (Fullan, 2007, p. 186). The potential for students to be thoughtful contributors should not be surprising; after all, students spend significant portions of everyday observing teaching and participating in (or sometimes avoiding) learning. Researchers Jones and Yonezawa note, "Students have unique expertise regarding schools and can provide important information about school and classroom practices and policies" (2008–2009, p. 66). Their work has demonstrated that when students are involved, reform is often more responsive, sustainable, and impactful.

One of the beautiful elements of AR is that it pushes us to prioritize student voice in our classrooms. It provides a space to listen to our students and to be more transparent about our own practice. It encourages us to shift the authority in the classroom, to step out from behind the teacher's desk and engage with the students in the process of thinking together about how to strengthen the learning experience in the classroom.

The chapters that follow share stories of teachers listening to and learning from students' voices while engaged in action research. We begin with Melissa Han's account of engaging with the voices of her 1st grade students. Melissa's action research was designed to explore how teaching and learning might be transformed in her classroom if she focused in on asking for direct student input. The lessons she learned from her 6- and 7-year-olds present a compelling case for the power of student voice.

Jessica De Young Kander then shared her account of nervously revealing to her college-age students that she planned to investigate her practice, a revelation necessitated by the permissions forms required as part of the IRB process. Jessica initially worried that acknowledging that her teaching could be improved would lead students to lose faith in her authority. However, taking the brave step of asking for student input prompted her to recognize that being transparent creates a space for honest and productive dialogue that can strengthen practice and deepen fulfillment for both teacher and students.

Tony Spitzberg's chapter shows a research project that stalled and caused significant frustration both for him as a teacher researcher and for his middle school students, until he began to elicit his students' input and learn from their suggestions. His experience demonstrates both the beauty and the challenge of engaging in a research process that is dynamic and interactive. Unlike the cookie-cutter science projects that many of us completed for our 5th grade science fairs, AR doesn't have a predetermined outcome, and it is often only by listening to students that we truly learn from the experience.

The final two chapters in this section explore the challenges of letting go of control and allowing student voices to have an authentic presence in the action research process. First, Makeba Jones describes a participatory action research project with high school students looking at reforms within their own schools. Although the project was specifically designed to engage student voices, when the students landed on a topic that Makeba recognized as politically charged, she hesitated out of concern for both student interests and her own reputation in the community. Similarly, Stacey Williams, working with university students, set out to design her AR project to encourage co-creation of learning but also found it hard to move out of the traditional teacher-student authority structure. In her chapter, Stacey provides some great tips and guiding questions for avoiding "power hoarding" and engaging student voices.

As you read the accounts presented here, here are a few questions to consider as you think about your own teaching and research:

- How do each of these authors engage student voice in their research? How does student voice inform their practice?
- What does student voice mean to you? How do you currently access it to inform your own practice? How might you?
- What is an issue you are struggling with or wondering about? How could you solicit feedback from students, or engage them as thought partners, to help you understand the issue better and to generate possible next steps?

- Whose voices are most present in your classroom or school? Whose voices would you like to hear more? How can you create opportunities for all students to be heard in your classroom or school? How can you ensure diverse perspectives in your research?
- How might you engage student voice in your own research? What would it look like for students to become collaborators in your research?

WORKS CITED

Fullan, M. (2007). *The new meaning of educational change* (4th ed.). New York: Routledge.

Jones, M., & Yonezawa, S. (2008, December–2009, January). Student-driven research. *Educational Leadership, 66*(4), 65–69.

Joselowsky, F. (2005). Students as co-constructors of the learning experience and environment: Youth engagement and high school reform. *Voices in Urban Education: High School Redesign, 8*, 12–22.

Yonezawa, S., & Jones, M. (2009, Summer). Student voices: Generating reform from the inside out. *Theory into Practice, 48*(3), 205–212.

CHAPTER FOURTEEN

Learning to Listen

MELISSA HAN

I confess. I am a recovering control freak.

My initial ideals about teaching were reduced to controlling my students in an effort to motivate them to care about the work we were doing. My methods went from bribing—"Those who complete this assignment will get a prize out of the prize box"—to threats—"If you don't finish this on time, you'll lose recess." This was the battle I had with my students year after year. My conversations in the teachers' workroom took on the tone of self-pity and blame. If I was teaching them what to learn and how to learn it, then why were the blank stares still there? Why were they regurgitating statements in class instead of saying what they were actually thinking? If I was working so hard, then why did I still have to convince them to do the work? The reality is that my students' actions reflected my own. We were both uninspired, and I felt defeated.

Instead of being their mentor and advocate, I was perpetuating a system that controlled student thinking and feeling, in the name of what we called learning. I believed that if my students appeared calm and quiet, said the appropriate statements in class, and performed well on standardized tests, then they were internalizing what we learned. The opposite was happening. The same students were still falling behind, and those who weren't became bored. This had to stop. I had to go back to the beginning and discover how to live out being the kind of educator I had dreamed to be.

I decided to create an educational experience for students that matched the sense of democracy and empowerment I hoped for when I began teaching. Instead of keeping control, I sought to empower my students through the pursuit of the research question "What happens when student voice and student reflection guide my teaching and our learning?" During this pursuit I redefined my role as teacher, enabling my students to know themselves and each other well as learners through a collaborative culture. My hope was that through this process, we would learn how to listen actively, ask questions, and create space for students' voices to guide how we learn within a democratic classroom, ultimately empowering the students as individuals.

At the beginning of the research process, I began to see that my research would involve more than my students. It would involve researching my own journey, my own transformation. The process of change involves rough spots. We developed our class through navigating these rough spots—moments when voices wanted to be heard, including the voice of a teacher who was learning how to listen instead of control. Listening is a skill that develops and strengthens with practice. Over time, I learned to listen and respond so that my students would be empowered by *their* voices to define learning that was meaningful to them. I challenged myself to listen more to the voices of my students and less to the voices that reminded me about tests and performance. In doing so, I found that my 1st grade students wanted me to be mindful of some key ideas.

COMPLIANCE IS NOT LEARNING

Each year, I ran into students who were difficult to reach and those who seemed easier to reach. I couldn't help but wonder why the hardest to reach students looked and sounded the same across grade levels at my school. We know who the hardest to reach students are. They are the ones who take up the most energy. They are angry and defiant, or quiet and behind. Both are hardest to reach because they have checked out of learning in our classrooms. In my research, I chose Andy and Anna as two of my four focus students because they had these qualities. It was time to reach out and create a learning environment that would work for them.

We have all had an Andy. Andy already had a record of anger and noncompliance at the tender age of six. In the past, I have felt threatened when students acted out in these ways, so I controlled more. As a result, students would check out. Why make an effort if it was impossible to succeed with me, their controlling teacher? I knew from my reading that anger and noncompliance usually emerge in children from feelings of unjustness (Assor et al., 2005). I also knew I had to act against my instincts to control Andy through behavior contracts and punishments, and instead ask him what was uncomfortable and how to change it. I chose to see his outbursts as opportunities rather than attempts to challenge me to a power struggle. He was asking me good questions—questions that pushed me to be more explicit about what we were doing and why it was meaningful. Becoming more explicit about our purpose and the steps along the way benefitted not just Andy—it benefitted all of my students.

Anna, on the other hand, was quiet. Unlike Andy, she did not speak up when she didn't understand what she was learning. As a result, she was often left behind. Tuning out, anxiety, and anger are all signals that indicate that a student's need for autonomy is being threatened (Assor et al., 2005). Anna helped me realize that all children need to be given choices and safe opportunities to voice what they need. If I was to reach students like Andy and Anna, I needed to use their feedback to guide our learning. As I repeatedly asked Andy and Anna questions about what was comfortable and uncomfortable, and implemented their ideas, they both were eager to share more. It was as if they had been waiting for an opportunity to say what they thought.

Surprisingly, when I asked the same questions of my easier to reach students, I had a different experience. The easier to reach students in our school are those who do as they are told without being asked twice. They are the ones who perform well on tests and are the first to receive academic awards. Charlie and Abbey were those easier to reach students for me because they were compliant. They responded well to control. Yet, when I asked them what was uncomfortable and how they would like to change the way we learn, they had the most difficulty answering those questions. I realized that compliance is a mirage. It may have seemed that I was reaching my compliant students because they were well behaved and were doing their work. But according to Assor and colleagues, they might have been just doing what they are told (2005). In actuality, I may not be reaching them, because they do not have their own internal motivation to learn. Instead of focusing on learning, they are distracted by pleasing the teacher or looking smart.

Andy, Anna, Charlie, and Abbey taught me that teacher-centered classrooms—where the teacher dictates what, how, and when students should learn—don't work for them. When students experience a teacher-centered classroom, they tend to act out, shut down, or comply. When students experience a student-centered classroom where their ideas and questions are taken seriously, they develop the confidence to persevere in the face of challenges, rely on one another, and create innovative solutions. This happened when I asked questions and truly listened to what my students said.

TEACHERS DON'T SEE EVERYTHING, SO ASK THE STUDENTS

I used to think that I knew everything that happened in my classroom. After witnessing the same students falling behind, and the same students who I thought had grasped what we learned forgetting, I realized that I didn't always know what was happening in my class, or why. I decided to ask the students.

However, a typical survey or set of interview questions wouldn't do with 1st graders. I discovered that the best way to find out what my 1st graders thought was to talk to them while they played. In our early "play interviews" I learned that writing was uncomfortable for my students. Although Andy was comfortable vocalizing his discomfort ("Ahh! Why?! Writing is boring!"), others responded to the discomfort in quieter ways, like walking to the opposite end of the room to poke another student instead of completing their writing. Their behavior signaled that they felt the same as Andy, and in our play conversations they were able to share their discomfort with me directly.

When I asked my students what would help writing feel better, their response was simple. They wanted choices about what they could write with (pencils or markers) and where they could write (sitting or standing at their desks or lying down on the rug). After we implemented their suggestions, I saw students write carefully and take their time thinking about what they wanted to say. Writing is more involved than choosing a writing tool, but the motivation to write emerged when they felt physically comfortable.

This was an "Aha!" moment for me. My students knew what would help them feel comfortable to learn. In the past, I would have relied on bribing with rewards and punishing by withholding recess to encourage them to write more. I realized that my former methods made my students resist even more whatever we were learning. The act of asking questions, listening, and responding to what students said gave them an entry point to learn.

I also learned that the acts of asking, listening, and responding needed to happen all the time. My students and I began a Being Curious George project where students chose research topics they were curious about. They collaborated in teams to research their own questions and design pages in a picture book to teach kindergarteners about their topics. During writing time, I noticed my students were struggling to write sentences in their paragraphs. Yet, no one was asking for help. When I shared that I noticed that they had some challenges in writing, they began to openly discuss what their challenges were. I then asked them what they needed help with on exit cards so that my quieter students would feel comfortable to share. The majority of my students said they needed more time to learn how to turn sentences from their research into paragraphs. They also asked to have their 5th grade buddies help critique their writing for our project.

This listening and responding process made me realize that students care about their work too. I had to trust my students and slow down to respond to what they said they needed. This was difficult. I felt pressure to cover all the standards before the end of the year, but I also wanted my students to learn skills that foster deeper knowledge. I found that when I slowed down, trusted my students' voices, and taught what my students said they needed more time to learn, they were more invested in what we were learning. Then "moving on" was easier because they had the foundation to build on. Even at a young age, students know what feels good and what doesn't. I needed to trust them to guide the class. I also needed to trust them to solve their own problems.

GIVE STUDENTS THE FREEDOM AND TRUST TO SOLVE THEIR OWN PROBLEMS

Year after year, I continued to witness the same students disengage from school and the same few praised. I realized that since I was the one telling my students when they were behaving or not working hard enough, by moving their behavior clip or taking away their recess, they never learned how to monitor themselves. Kohn (1993) states that we must allow students to have power with authentic choices, and guide them in how to handle that responsibility. I decided to put away my behavior chart and erase the table points. Instead, I decided to rely on three structures:

- *Community Meetings* where the whole class would come together to reflect, acknowledge each other, discuss problems, and identify potential solutions.
- *A Private Conversation Table* where students could invite each other to have a private conversation about a problem they experienced. Together we generated sentence starters and norms that were posted on this table to guide the conversations.
- *Three Feedback Boxes* around the room where students could contribute their ideas for Problems to Solve, Ideas for Change, and Celebrations.

During my research I read that A. S. Neill, who founded the Summerhill School in England, designed a system in which students practiced democracy through community meetings. My role during our community meetings was to guide my students to speak and listen to each other while working through a problem. I also asked them to share solution ideas that students with problems could choose from and try for a week. I found that my students' ideas were more creative than what I would have suggested. I also noticed that the students would listen to each other's problems because they had a purpose—to contribute ideas to help our community function more efficiently and peacefully. I was often fascinated by my students' bluntness and honesty with each other. Those were times when it was difficult for me to bite my tongue and not say anything. There were also times that I needed to step in. However, instead of sharing my idea, I would ask the group a question, hoping that it would lead them to a helpful solution.

For example, during our Being Curious George project, some of the teams were having trouble collaborating. Abbey was frustrated that her team was not doing the work to finish their page in our picture book. When I asked her what she thought should be done, she suggested that each person have a role and that the roles rotate each day. The class was willing to try this, and found the idea very helpful.

WHEN STUDENTS HAVE CHOICE, YOU DON'T HAVE TO CONVINCE THEM TO LEARN

When students have choice, they take the work home, they have a reason for engaging with their peers, they feel listened to, and they enjoy it more, even when the work is harder. I discovered this when my students and I did our Being Curious George project. At the end of each year my colleagues and I talk with regret about what we would have taught if we didn't need to worry about benchmark assessments or other standardized tests. During my research year, I made the decision to discover what my 1st grade students were curious about and turn it into a project.

We used our Curiosity Wall, a designated place in our room, to collect student questions and passions that they wanted to delve deeper into. We then formed teams of students who had similar curiosities. Each team chose the question that would guide their research. At first, I was going to have each student create a product and exhibit their project in whatever way they chose. But due to the variety of amazing ideas my students shared, I was worried that I wouldn't be able to provide the structures they needed to finish their products. I shared my worries with my students and proposed that we create a picture book. I asked them to choose an audience to whom they wanted to teach their knowledge, and they chose kindergartners.

Throughout the project, my students kept the kindergarten audience in mind in the choices they made while designing the book and planning our exhibition. These choices mattered because they had an audience. They wanted to be good teachers and they knew their information needed to be accurate and engaging. My young 1st graders held each other accountable and offered helpful feedback to each other during critique sessions with their work. We became what Rogoff refers to as a community of learners:

> [I]n a community of learners classroom … [there are] complex group relations among class members who learn to take responsibility for their contribution to their own learning and to the group's functioning. Instead of one individual trying to control and address 30 students at once, it is a community working together with all serving as resources to the others. (1994, p. 214)

Parents of my students told me that their child shared with excitement what they were learning in their project once they got home. One mother called me to say that her child was sick and couldn't come to school, but was mad at her because he was missing project time. During the Being Curious George project, I didn't formally invite parents to our exhibition since my students chose to have kindergartners as our audience. And yet I was receiving texts and emails from families asking when our exhibition was because their child was inviting them to come, too. In the past, I had to tell parents what we were learning because my students didn't remember, or didn't feel it was relevant enough to share. Having choice made students feel invested in their learning, and they wanted to share it.

LISTENING TRANSFORMS US

This process of listening and responding was crucial in building trust with my students since their voices were guiding us. I wanted students to feel comfortable asking questions, reflecting on what they learned, and sharing how they learned best. I also wanted them to use their voices to advocate for one another and strengthen our community. Relying on student voice filled me with tensions that I needed to press through. There were times when I wanted to abandon relying on student voice and go back to controlling. There were times when the research process brought out the ugliness in me.

At times, I felt like I was going through control withdrawal. I was afraid of the unpredictable. I was afraid of failing. I constantly doubted if it would work. I was grumpy. It felt as if I was a beginning teacher all over again. At one point, out of my weakness, I caved and used table points to make my students listen to me instead of discussing with them solutions to our problems. I realize now that I didn't trust my students and I didn't trust myself. Instead of giving up, I used this moment to reflect on why I made that decision in the first place, why this was hard for me, and to connect back to the hopes and goals I had for my research. I also learned that it was important that I was honest with my students, admitting when I had made mistakes and engaging my students to help correct them. I was beginning to believe that perceived mistakes, like the table points, were critical in helping me go deeper with what I was truly after in my research.

At that moment, I realized what the action in action research meant. It wasn't figuring it all out from the beginning. The research journey is filled with endless questions, failures, and triumphs. All of them inform further action. This process was repeated throughout the research. I now see that it was helpful to have a skeleton of the research design from the beginning, but it was more important to be open to the unexpected paths that end up being beautiful accidents. I needed to be present in the moment, whatever it would be. Those moments were the right moments that needed to happen, because they led me on a journey of discovery with my students. It was then that I decided to surrender to the research process. It was then that I believed my students would teach me what they knew all along to be relevant for their learning experiences.

After this awareness, I stopped being afraid of the unexpected. I welcomed it. It was then that I discovered who my reachable and unreachable focus students were during their student-led conferences. I began to recognize my students as windows to helping me understand what learning was like for them. I began to see how my research would go beyond my own classroom and inform the issues my school was struggling with, and education at large. I realized that my reachable and unreachable students represented the students at my school, at any school. If I found that listening to student voice and providing choice would reach *my* students, then this was true for *all* of our students.

In the end, just as I had needed to surrender to the research process, I had to approach writing up my research in a similar way. I wrote uninhibitedly so that I could arrive at what I really wanted to say. I wrote in a style that I would want read. I stopped writing to prove something, and instead wrote to share an experience. I wrote to reveal my vulnerability, my questions, my doubts, and my failures. And most of all, I wrote to share my students' voices. I am part of a community with other researchers who have come before me. I am building my research on their knowledge. There will be others who will come after me to build on what I have learned. I am convinced that action research is how we educators should approach learning with students on a daily basis. The process enables all of us to get to the heart of learning for all students. We are building understanding together—seeking to understand our students so that they may all be reached, and we may be transformed.

WORKS CITED

Assor, A., Kaplan, H., Kanat-Maymon, Y., & Roth, G. (2005). Directly controlling teacher behaviors as predictors of poor motivation and engagement in girls and boys: The role of anger and anxiety. *Learning and Instruction, 15*(5), 397–413.

Kohn, A. (1993, September). Choices for children: Why and how to let students decide. *Phi Delta Kappan, 75*(1), 8–20. Retrieved November 8, 2011, from http://www.alfiekohn.org/teaching/cfc.htm

Rogoff, B. (1994, Fall). Developing understanding of the idea of communities of learners. *Mind, Culture, and Activity, 1*(4), 209–229.

CHAPTER FIFTEEN

Letting Students See BEHIND THE Curtain

Transparency, Teacher as Learner, and the IRB

JESSICA DE YOUNG KANDER

Three years ago I let my students in on a dirty little secret: I don't always know what I'm doing 100% of the time. I admitted that I am still learning and growing. And as terrifying as it was to make this admission, it was also liberating. It transformed my work as a teacher, making me a better instructor and providing a stronger learning experience for my students.

I can see it in their eyes at the start of every semester; I look too young to be teaching college students. At the very most, I have a good 10 years on my students, but frequently, much less, and in some cases I am, indeed, younger. This was something I was so keenly aware of as a new teacher that I carefully constructed an impenetrable teaching persona. I wove together a persona that was as much a reflection of every Hollywood stereotype of academia as it was my own idealistic view of higher education. This constructed self necessitated that I always appeared in charge, unshakable, and as if I knew precisely what I was doing at every conceivable moment of every single interaction I had with every single student both in and out of the classroom, while simultaneously channeling a *Dead Poets Society* realness and approachability. Not only was this model of teaching persona unrealistic, it was exhausting. However, I didn't fully realize this until my 4th semester of teaching.

We teachers bandy around the term *burnout* as a catch-all description of what many of us experience at some point during our teaching careers. I refused, early on, to let this malady get me down. I would rise above burnout. I would survive. I would. Oh, who was I kidding? Four semesters into teaching in a college setting and I was ready to throw in the towel. While the comics would have you believe that all problems can be solved by a caped or masked superhero, it was just your average teacher research group that saved me.

The teacher research group that I joined after 2 years of teaching is an extension of our local chapter of the National Writing Project. The group is made up of teachers who are committed to learning about and conducting classroom-based research. This particular group has been active for more than a decade, with members each using their own research studies to create changes in their classrooms. And boy, did I need a change. I found myself, after a mere month in the group, plunging headfirst into restructuring the assessments I was using (traditional exams and essays) in the hopes that I might discover better classroom dynamics, more authentic instruction and discussions, and, hopefully, a resurgence of my passion for teaching.

To better understand how my restructuring was working, I began to collect student artifacts, survey students, and conduct individual interviews. As is the case with most action research—research involving human subjects (in this case, my students)—this meant paperwork. I needed to have my research approved by my university's Institutional Review Board (IRB). An IRB is a committee that exists to approve, monitor, and review research involving human subjects in order to protect the subjects from physical or psychological harm.

In order to have my research approved by the IRB, I needed to obtain consent from my students. I accomplished this by creating an informed consent form. This form explained to the students what I was hoping to accomplish in my research, the methods I would use, and what their involvement would be in said research. Additionally, the form provided assurances for my students that there would be no negative consequences for choosing not to be involved. Students would sign the form, either giving their consent to be involved in my research or requesting to be excluded.

Rather than simply asking for vague permission to use their work and elicit their responses in surveys and interviews, I chose the route of transparency. This was, for a young teacher with a heavily guarded persona, a terrifying prospect. I had to admit to my students that I was (a) trying something new and (b) didn't know everything. I started class by passing out the consent forms. I hesitantly came clean about participating in a teacher research group outside of school and described, in detail, my research project. I remember I was leaning on the edge of my lectern because I felt shaky from nerves and wasn't sure I could keep my composure without the solid wood table holding me up. I gulped in air and began. I was expecting my students to either zone out and show blatant disinterest or, in my worst-case scenario playbook, call me out as not really knowing what I was doing. I hadn't even considered the possibility of enthusiastic interest. I had set aside a mere 5 minutes of class time to explain the project, go over what the student involvement would be, and answer any questions. Almost 35 minutes later, I had to cut off the class discussion and questions that had unexpectedly arisen. Several of my students wanted to know more about the research group I was a part of and asked me to elaborate on what we did in the group meetings, while several other students seemed concerned that I might be using these teacher research sessions to complain about them. I quickly assured them that we generally focused on our teaching and not on our students. and the few times students did come up in more than a general way, it was to highlight something amazing or wonderful they had done. Other students were genuinely excited to hear that I, someone with two master's degrees who was, in their estimation, far beyond school, could still be looking for opportunities to learn. One student with his own aspirations of going on to teach asked me if this was a group he could join when he graduated in a year.

That day I had a handful of students stick around at the end of class to talk more about both the research project and the teacher research group. I was, to put it mildly, shocked. Rather than questioning my authority and knowledge, my students seemed to have gained a new respect for me as their instructor. They were not concerned with my roundabout admission that I did not know what I was doing. Instead, they seemed oddly at ease about this fact. More students spoke up during class discussions that week. My favorite moment was when a student stopped a whole class discussion because he needed help understanding an idea another student had presented. He self-confidently admitted that it was something he had never considered before and that he wasn't sure he agreed, but wanted to know more. Additionally, I gained a small entourage as I moved from our classroom to my office at the end of class each day, who were always asking me questions or reflecting on my teaching and/or my research.

I found over the next several weeks that I became more transparent in most aspects of my teaching. I was explaining, not defending (as I had previously feared I might end up doing), my teaching decisions, from how I was breaking students into groups to why I was asking them particular questions on the reading quizzes. And what's more, my students were responding with overwhelming enthusiasm. The feedback I got from my students was not always glowing, I should be sure that I make that clear. They often had criticisms of assignments, lessons, and readings. For instance, a few students chatting with me after class one afternoon pointed out that they understood why I had included a particular reading on our course reading list, but suggested that perhaps I could simply cover the material from the reading in class and instead have them read more specific example texts to which they could apply these new concepts. And you know what? They were absolutely right! Rather than feeling as if they were attacking me, I felt like we were entering into a genuine conversation where we accepted that we had something to learn from each other.

My students seemed to gain a new respect for me after I opened up to them about my teacher research. That I was willing to admit I was still learning seemed to open the floodgates. My students appeared more willing to participate actively in their own learning. By inviting them into the research process as collaborators rather than merely participants, I found that my students became more analytical, both of my teaching and of their own learning. One student excitedly stated that she finally understood my propensity for beginning class with a think-pair-share that ended in a whole-class idea web on the board. She astutely pointed out that I was using this activity as a way to gauge what the students already knew, needed to know, and were either confused or misinformed about, allowing me to tailor our discussions to the specific needs of the class.

It became common, after introducing my research, for students to ask me questions about class activities and to provide their own insights on why it might help their learning (and how it might inform their own future teaching). A number of students commented that they felt more invested in their learning in my class than they previously had because they felt more comfortable working through ideas since they knew I was doing the same with my teaching. Nowhere was this more evident than in the overheard comment from a student one afternoon during a small group activity. The group was working diligently on their assignment when a young woman paused to state, "Okay, I have this little baby thought that I think fits our question. Maybe you guys can help me work through it?"

The control I was so scared of losing with my confession that I was not an all-knowing entity at the front of the room dissipated. I no longer lost sleep over constructing the perfect teaching persona. The process of confessing my own status as an imperfect human being who is still learning allowed my authentic self to shine through in my teaching, allowing me to keep teaching, semester after semester, year after year. Although I don't always ask my students to sign consent forms each time I begin a course, I do begin each course by drawing back the curtain and confessing that I too am still a learner. Do I still get flutters and nervous tremors before making this admission? Absolutely! After all, I am confronting both my and my students' perceptions about the role of teacher and students. However, I no longer feel that I'm jumping off a cliff into unknown territory. I've been down this path before, and I know that although there may be bumps along the way, the relationship with my students, their learning, and my own experience as a teacher will be so much richer for changing the dynamic and recognizing that we are all learning together.

CHAPTER SIXTEEN

It's Not ABOUT THE Technique

Learning That Teaching Is More Heart Than Strategy

TONY SPITZBERG

After observing in the classroom for what seemed like years, my cooperating teacher was going to hand his masterfully sculpted class of 6th graders to me. My enthusiasm and expectations knew no bounds. The class was about to start a fantastic new book, *Freak the Mighty*. For my action research project, I decided to pair the book with reading response journals, a technique we had read about in my teacher credential program and which my cooperating teacher strongly endorsed. My understanding was that these response journals encourage students to construct their own meaning from what they read, motiving them to make connections that would lead to understanding as well as an awareness of their own thinking, which improves their literacy skills. I had the books and the students had their journals. Let the literacy flow.

Visions of *Dead Poets Society* danced in my head. Starting off that first day of class, I imagined myself reading aloud to the group, inspiring them to write thoughtful and thought-provoking prose. I would take my students to new heights of self-expression, they would boldly read their writing to the applause of their classmates, and I would nod my head with grinning approval!

Things started incredibly well. We began reading the novel and the students enjoyed it as much as I had expected they would. They were engaged throughout the read-alouds and expressed their delight by constantly asking that we continue reading past the end of the class period.

We were several chapters into the book when I introduced the reading response journals. This is when my vision began to unravel. I told my students to write down quotes from the book that inspired them, and then instructed them to "simply" connect the quotes to their own lives with a few paragraphs of brilliant, meaningful thought. I handed them a sheet I had created that summarized these instructions with a brief list of possible sentence lead-ins.

That day we had read fewer chapters than usual, so the students were already unhappy when I introduced the journal assignment. However, I had wanted to leave plenty of time for them to write. So high were my expectations that I was actually concerned that 30 minutes of writing time wouldn't be enough. I beamed as they opened their journals to begin the assignment, feeling fortunate that I had such a colorful and creative group of students. I glowed as I wandered around the classroom, believing that soon I would read about deep and intimate aspects of their lives as they connected them to the novel. I would get to witness the golden process of inspirational literacy in the making! Maybe this activity would inspire them to become authors or playwrights. I was certain there must be at least one Shakespeare or Hemingway in the mix. At the very least, we would be able to celebrate together that through our journaling we had reached a deeper appreciation for the story and for each other as individuals with varied life experiences.

"How much do we have to write?"—one student's voice interrupted my reverie. My grin flattened immediately as I realized that most of the students had put their pencils down or were either doodling on the backs of their journals or chatting with their neighbors. It had been less than 5 minutes.

I plastered a smile on my face, hoping that perhaps the quality of their writing might outpace the duration. I asked a student to share what she had written in her journal, quieting everyone down and reminding them that we need to respect each others' ideas and experiences. "The quote I chose says that the main character's name is Max," the student read aloud from her journal. "I wrote that Max is nice and that there's a kid in my neighborhood named Max too. He's also nice." My heart sank. This was one of my top students. I'd seen her engage in discussions with insightful commentary and outstanding questions. And this was her response? Boring. Superficial. Totally uninspired. I felt like such a failure. "Um, Mr. Spitzberg," another student said as I stood there dumbfounded, "can't we just read?" Other students voiced their agreement that reading more would be best, and I nodded, realizing that my halcyon dream of a writer's utopia had come crashing down around me.

Over the next few days, I attempted to salvage the reading response journals. Having failed as an inspirational figure, I turned into a somewhat crazed cheerleader. I found myself darting around the classroom, peeking over students' shoulders and making comments like, "I know you can write more than that! Are you sure you're finished?," "What about that story you told during the discussion? Could you relate it to a quote?," and "You're already finished? How about picking a few more quotes?" Although I attempted to maintain a positive attitude, I found my frustration mounting. The response journals had become a struggle. My students and I were on opposite sides of a tug-of-war. The more I pushed, the more they resisted. I began to increase the number of quotes to which they had to respond and started pointing out quotes that I thought should be meaningful. Their complaining became more vocal. The 5-minute writing time remained. And even the book itself, the text they had loved, began to lose its luster as the negativity of the reading response journal experience spilled over onto *Freak the Mighty*.

Had it not been for my action research project, I would have readily discarded reading response journals and moved onto something else. But as a grad student engaged in action research through a combined master's degree and credential program, I had tied myself to an AR project focused on reading response journals, and I couldn't walk away.

My first few weeks of phase 1 data were abysmal. Both students' journal responses and their affective feedback were disappointing. I needed to do something to turn things around. Fortunately, spring break provided a reprieve for me to reflect, reassess, and refocus.

I began by rereading every piece of literature I could find about implementing response journals, and quickly realized that I had skipped over some important elements in my earlier literature review. As I had discovered in the classroom, simply passing out a guide, explaining it to students, and expecting them automatically to write with conviction was a mistake. This teacher-centered approach caused the students to remain dependent on me for direction and guidance. They had come to identify the function of response journals as a quick means of writing "correct answers."

When I started the action research process, I expected that it would help me to find specific pedagogical strategies that I could use to strengthen my teaching. However, as I reviewed my data and revisited the literature I became increasingly aware that focusing on strategies was not enough. By trying to distill teaching into a perfect formula, I had lost all of the fun and excitement that had characterized our classroom prior to starting my action research. I wasn't ready to give up reading response journals, but I needed to figure out how to make them meaningful for students. Instead of forcing the writing, how could I create the conditions that would make them want to write?

When we returned from break, I borrowed a suggestion from one of the articles I had reviewed and decided to write with the students. I had already established a reputation with the students as a funny writer, and so I decided to leverage that talent to get them to laugh a little and re-establish some of our classroom community. I related a part of that day's reading to a late-night face-to-face encounter I had had with a rather large and frightening koala bear while walking back to my hostel, alone in the Australian rainforest. The classroom thundered with laughter. I asked if anyone else wanted to share, and immediately, several hands went up. "So we can write funny things?" one student asked. "Of course," I replied, thinking I had told them this weeks ago, but realizing that telling hadn't been enough. I needed to show my students the power of response journals by writing alongside them. Ultimately, as I began to write and read my own entries, more students seemed willing—even enthusiastic—to share their own. A comfortable, and most importantly, trusting creative alliance was born!

As the class became more confident in their journal responses, I decided to give more responsibility to the students by having them create their own evaluation rubric. To get the conversation started, I created some nonexamples of poor journal responses on the board. Students thought these were funny and immediately recognized what was wrong. A few students mimicked these poor responses, creating funny nonexamples of their own; the class was full of laughter. Some students who felt they had effective examples read them to the class, and impressed, we included these in the rubric as well. This was one of the first times we truly enjoyed sharing writing together. However tentatively, we were becoming a community of writers.

As the class gained confidence and interest, students began to ask if they could compose their own writing prompts. Slightly awed, I responded with an enthusiastic "Yes!" They shared their prompts with each other and with me. They swapped ideas and provided critiques of each others' responses. Soon we barely had enough time during the writing segment of class for all who wanted to read what they had written. I knew we had reached a new high when they volunteered to read some of the book chapters at home so that we could have more time for response journals in class. There had truly been a transformation in the classroom.

I came to realize that students were no longer writing because they were supposed to, they were writing because they wanted to. They wanted to share their ideas. They wanted to impress their peers. The anticipation of what each person would read and the surprises that would surely come meant that, for these 6th graders, writing had taken on social capital. Writing well carried status, and everyone was expected to participate.

As we began to have fun with our reading response journal entries, the entire experience was enhanced. Students' understanding of the book increased, creativity and engagement multiplied, and we became more responsive to our community's writing needs. My role changed from that of a teacher trying to "get" them to write as I slowly became a person involved in the same task. They saw that I was trying as hard as they were to make sense of the events of the book in relation to a life that can be exciting, joyful, and heartbreaking for all of us.

After the semester was completed, the reading response journals returned home with the students, and with the last set of action research data collected, a clear turning point in the research stands out. It was only when I stopped trying to control the classroom, stopped trying to ferret out the perfect pedagogical formula, and stopped attempting to rely on reading response journals as a teaching technique that we were able to open a space for literacy to grow in the classroom. I had to stop trying to force success out of my action plan and instead learn to use AR as a framework to listen to students, build common goals, and explore ideas together. And I had to connect back to being a writer myself, to having fun with my writing and to sharing that joy with my students.

Would I have learned all this without AR? Maybe. I hope so. But I know that if I hadn't been actively engaged in the AR process I wouldn't have stuck with those reading response journals after students started to complain. I would have moved on to another technique, another pedagogical "fix." AR forced me to look hard at what was working, what wasn't, and *why*. It required me to go beyond technique to look at relationships and my role as a pivotal meaning maker between students and content. My AR project caused me massive amounts of stress, lost sleep, and headaches. But engaging in the process also led me to be a much better, more effective educator, a benefit well worth the cost.

CHAPTER SEVENTEEN

Youth-Led Action Research

A Lesson in Letting Go of Control

MAKEBA JONES

The high school students had just arrived at the university where I work. We walked to my office and settled into the nearby conference room. I was facilitating a training of student action researchers who would design and conduct educational research at their high school. While snacking on bagels and cream cheese, we introduced ourselves. I then described the agenda for the day and introduced the research process. I always invite students into the research process by asking them to discuss their educational experiences and their relationships with adults in their high school. The discussion helps the group identify important problems and dilemmas from which to pull research questions for their study. Students were animated in the conference room chairs as they talked about their experiences in classrooms and at the school overall. Their energy was palpable and seemed to fill the conference room. The novice researchers were starting to gel as a team as they bonded over shared experiences and perspectives about the quality of education at their high school. This was an important part of the process because students take the lead on all aspects of the research, which means they need to function as a team. Students needed to own the work, and my role was to support their process and experience. But that morning in the conference room, something happened that caught me off guard. I was not prepared for the turn in the students' discussion or my reaction.

A few students in the group excitedly suggested that the team investigate the school's budget and, specifically, how the principal spends the budget. The team quickly pounced on the idea, agreeing unanimously. Their interest in the school budget was not unreasonable. Recent state budget cuts prompted districts and schools to lay off teachers and cut student support programs. Students were upset that their school had fewer resources than in prior years. They felt their educational achievement was compromised without these resources. However, in that moment I was focused on myself. I could not hear what they were saying.

Through a university-based program, I ran a number of youth voice action research projects. I worked with high school students to share with teachers and administrators their perspectives about their educational experiences. I advocated that their voices were heard by the adults in the school and that school leaders leverage students' perspectives to make changes in the school. At the time, I worked with several schools in one district on youth-led action research where students designed and conducted research and then shared the results with teachers and administrators. I worried that my reputation as an education ally would be damaged if I allowed the research team to investigate how the principal spends the school's budget. I remember the sound of students' voices fading as a heavy pit grew in my stomach. My attention drifted as I imagined my worst nightmare: the principal kicking me out of the school and rallying other principals in the district to refuse to work with me. When I came back to consciousness, I stammered a few vague responses such as "We'll see" and "I don't know. There might be privacy issues." I was stalling until I could figure out how to persuade the team to investigate a different topic.

For several years I ran student voice projects where youth were experts about needed reform at their high schools. Through interviews and focus groups, students discussed their educational experiences and conducted presentations to their school about educational insights from their experiences. Although I am a university researcher, my professional motivation is to always bridge research and practice. These worlds are often so far apart, and that never made sense to me. In my 15 years in education, I have always worked "in the middle" of research and practice, largely through close collaborations with teachers, parents, students, and administrators to create new and sustain existing supports for students. Even with several years of doing youth voice work, I was not prepared for the lesson I learned that day in the conference room. I was pushed to question my role in action research that is driven by youth. I had to confront and clarify my power and authority to shape the research. In my prior youth voice projects, I interviewed students, chose the topics students examined, and controlled how the information was presented to teachers and administrators. In my projects where youth drive the action research, youth make all the decisions about the research. But should they? I felt awful that morning for asking myself this question. The question reflected my uneasiness with my power and authority being challenged.

LEARNING TO LET GO OF CONTROL

After what seemed like an hour (really, several minutes) the shock wore off and I came to my senses. I admit shamefully that my first instinct was to use my authority as the adult "in charge" and say no to the team investigating the school budget. Instead, I listened to my instincts about how to proceed. I needed to hear the students. I asked why they believed the research topic was so important. Students talked freely about their frustrations with dwindling after-school support. Several students brought up mathematics specifically. Math was particularly difficult for many of them. The school used to have an after-school math support program to help students. I could hear the urgency in students' voices.

I listened quietly. I only interjected occasionally, to ask clarifying questions to help me understand the students' point of view. I asked the team if they were interested in investigating the school's budget, or if they were more interested in understanding the school's budget for support programs. This question opened up space for a conversation about how the school might continue supporting students' progress in math without the after-school program. The team was curious about the principal's plan to work around the budget cuts so that students continued receiving math support. The urgency in students' voices changed to excitement. They wanted to study math support resources at their school. The team was thrilled about the potential impact of their research on students' academic success.

The epiphany hit me as I watched students' energetic discussion. My relationship to the research is different in youth-led work. I have to let go, step back, and stop driving the research. My role is to support and guide the students who are driving the research. Youth-led action research is as much about youth's experiences as it is about the actual research. Students learned something critically important by zooming in on their own experiences to connect with meaningful educational issues, and then zooming out to look at the relevance of those issues to other students on the research team and in the school overall. If I had controlled the direction and flow of students' research ideas, I would have shortchanged students on learning the importance of shifting vantage points in the research process. My ego led me to temporarily forget that leadership development is fundamental in youth-led action research. Students learn important skills of critical thinking, critical questioning, cooperative learning and meaning making, democratic decision making, and self-advocacy. In that moment, I knew I needed to get out of the students' way, so I did. I voiced my support for their research focus. We then moved on to discussing the next steps in their research.

STEPPING IN AND OUT OF YOUTH'S RESEARCH

My epiphany clarified my two primary responsibilities in youth-led action research. Both responsibilities have little to do with me or the actual research. My responsibilities are youth-centered. They are: (1) setting up an authentic research experience where students choose to investigate real educational issues that affect them, and (2) actively encouraging students to take on new identities as novice researchers and leaders.

Setting up an authentic research experience means I think about the setting in which youth work. I don't mean the physical setting. For me, the setting is an interactional space that occurs as students work together. Student research teams that work well are committed to the project from start to finish because of a shared purpose. I model learning and working collaboratively as I teach them about the research process, tools of investigation and analysis, and research ethics. For all phases of the research process I draw on students' voices about their experiences in schools. Grounding the team's research training in their everyday experiences allows me to support emerging shared understandings about important educational problems to investigate.

Actively encouraging students to take on new identities means I think carefully about my relationships with the students. I want to stand back and support students' direction for the work. Yet, I also want to push them to behave outside their comfort zone. Knowing when to stand back or step forward means I need strong relationships with the students. When I know my students, I can gently persuade them to take risks. Every interaction is an opportunity for me to help students extend their reach.

I learned to enact these responsibilities by moving among the roles of teacher, coach, and facilitator. I directed, organized, supported, guided, suggested, motivated, cajoled, listened, and observed throughout the students' research process. Each meeting, I did several if not all of these. These multiple behaviors allowed me to step in and out of students' research. By my doing so, not only did students take risks and grow, but their unique "insider" perspective about the relationship between classroom life and student engagement was apparent throughout every stage of the research process. From the kinds of interview questions they thought to ask students and teachers to the way they could easily establish rapport with students they interviewed, involving student researchers can deepen the work of teacher researchers. A shared purpose of creating optimum learning experiences through joint action research can strengthen teacher-student relationships and student motivation to learn. Students appreciate and value being asked to participate in improving their education.

In my work, it took me time to become comfortable with stepping back. In the early days of my youth-driven research, sometimes I had to stuff my anxiousness as students led the way. One team in particular was a test of my internal resolve. While brainstorming important problems and issues to investigate, the African American and Latino students on the team brought up conceptions of race in the school. They talked at length about the ways in which students' perceptions impacted peer relationships and overall campus climate. Several students shared personal experiences of being the target of peers' racial jabs. Their self-esteem and sense of safety were jarred by the hurtful comments. The team was curious if their individual experiences were representative of a larger problem among students on campus. They wanted to survey all students in the high school about their conceptions of race and stereotypes about racial groups. This time, I did not go into shock at the idea! I supported the suggestion, knowing in the back of my mind that some students and teachers might be offended by the survey. We talked as a team about possible backlash and its effect on them. Students shared concerns about being alienated by their peers. But their commitment to the research outweighed their concerns. I worried that a backlash would douse students' sense of agency about improving their school. I feared the negative experience would silence them. Internally, I anxiously gripped my fears as I stayed back to support the team.

Once the team administered the survey, teachers and students resisted mildly. One teacher sent an email criticizing the appropriateness of the survey. She also questioned the validity of the research overall because of the survey's focus on race. A few students returned their surveys with written messages to the team such as "racist." In the end, I saw I had worried unnecessarily. The research team was pleased by the resistance. The students believed that the survey spurred conversations about race among students and faculty that might not have happened otherwise. They were not worried about backlash from peers because they were thrilled that their survey unearthed issues that were rarely discussed in the school.

I learned that their investment in and ownership of the action research strengthened their convictions about addressing the campus's racial climate. Although I might not have structured their action research in the same way because of my own concerns, by staying in the background I witnessed students embracing their identities as novice action researchers. They were resolved to tackle a dilemma that they believed weakened relationships among students and hampered peer interactions in classrooms. Only when I let go of control could the students grow. On the day of the presentation to teachers and administrators, the students' growth was visible. Students who started the research process a little shy and reticent about voicing their ideas spoke with authority about their research and the critical importance of their research results. They had developed into leaders with solid critical thinking and analytic skills about tough educational issues. In those moments watching them present their action research with straight backs and heads held high, I was so grateful I put students' voices ahead of my ego. Had I not, I would have prevented students, inadvertently, from investigating important issues that affect the quality of their education.

CHAPTER EIGHTEEN

Power Sharing or Power Hoarding? Reflections on My Position within the Research

STACEY WILLIAMS

Early on in my action research process, I sat in a meeting with my students discussing the topic of our research (social justice) as two students debated different perspectives on racial identity. I had just read an article that spoke to the exact dynamic being enacted in their debate, and I was exhilarated to see the theory come to life. In my excitement, I interrupted their conversation, explained "what was going on" through this theoretical lens, and started mapping out the theory on the board. As I drew the model, the students' interest, investment, and own perspectives deflated. By the time I had finished my tirade, the energy from the conversation was dead and the looks on my students' faces said they had no idea what to do with my interjection or whiteboard scribbles.

This moment is one of countless that point to a key tension I discovered in being the authority figure in the room (and person initiating the research) while also wanting to engage students in a research and learning process that honored and relied on their own knowledge and experience. While my research spoke of using power sharing and co-creation of theory, I frequently did not live up to this ideal.

During my action research project, I served as the interim director and graduate assistant at the University of San Diego's Women's Center. In these roles, I taught and advised student workers and volunteers leading programming around issues that disproportionately impact women. With this, my focus was on the leadership development of our student staff.

Within the context of student-advisor and student-teacher relationships, action research can be especially tricky. I found that it required great attention to my own positionality and power. Throughout the process, so many questions came up for me in terms of how to design my research given my position as researcher and professional working with students. All of this was further complicated by the fact that I was not only the principle investigator, but also completing action research as a requirement for my degree. Given these things, how voluntary did the research feel to my students? Did they feel like they had the space and choice to decline to participate? When most action taken was embedded into the work and life of our office, how clear were the boundaries for those who were disinterested? Beyond questions of participation, I wondered if they felt that they could give voice to their opinions and ideas, particularly if they were not in line with the dominant narrative of the group. Moreover, I was concerned about whether they felt agency to move the direction or focus of the research itself.

Both the formal and implicit power dynamics made shared ownership a complex web to navigate. I found that there were three questions I needed to repeatedly ask myself as I designed and implemented my project:

1. How am I sharing the work?
2. How am I thinking about my students?
3. How am I carrying my authority?

HOW AM I SHARING THE WORK?

My research posed the question "How do we engage social justice at the Women's Center?" During staff orientation, I explained my initial research question and desire to co-create the journey, inviting students to volunteer to participate. To begin, I thought of my first cycle as a sort of organizational needs assessment, and planned on interviewing students and staff to get a feel for how we currently understood social justice and what they thought would improve our learning. In my third interview with a student, I realized how misaligned this method was. Although *I* was learning a lot about our current approach to social justice, no one else was involved in the process. I was inadvertently positioning myself as the "keeper of knowledge." Because these interviews were individual, students were not able to share their experiences with others or hear others' perspectives. With this realization, I ended individual interviews, and we moved to a design that used group dialogue within every cycle.

At every step of the way, it was important for me to examine how I was sharing the process of the research. When we moved to using group dialogue, we also began a practice of shared note taking. With this technique, every student got a large piece of paper and access to markers scattered around, and we all tracked significant themes, ideas, and quotes that stood out. This change made it so that I was not solely in control of what was being recorded; instead, we shared the responsibility of collecting data. It also made for beautiful data!

Figure 1. Shared note taking from cycle 2. Photo by S. Williams.

While this was a good start, I again faced the trap of controlling the research when I took all of the shared notes and thought that I would analyze them by myself. Fortunately, one student asked me what I planned to do with the notes, and made it clear that we needed to look at them together. We made a gallery with the shared notes from all of our cycles and then engaged in a dialogue in which we collectively analyzed the data (again, taking shared notes to track our findings). With my concluding cycle, I then brought to the students how I planned on presenting our analysis and, in focus groups, asked, "How does this match up—or fail to capture—your experience? What works? What needs to change?"

Particularly given the already present power dynamics resulting from my position as advisor and instructor, I found that I had to be diligent in always asking for—and affirming the value of—students' knowledge. Considering *sharing* was an important piece of this; another that had a significant impact on my use of power was being thoughtful about my concept of my students.

HOW AM I THINKING ABOUT MY STUDENTS?

An important piece of avoiding the pitfalls of power hoarding was to critically examine how I viewed the students. Throughout the first cycle, I often found myself thinking of my students as repositories of information—relying on what Freire

(2000) calls the "banking model" of education, where I (the teacher) am simply depositing my knowledge *into* my students. I constantly caught myself thinking that I had some magic key or right answer that I needed to use to "enlighten" my students, or at least that I was somehow further "ahead" than they were.

My approach to planning our fall student training illustrates this type of thinking. I created the outline and topics for the entire program, as well as chose the book we read, selected the speakers, and wrote all of the reflection questions. The problem with this became most evident while I was planning a specific activity looking at the connections and distinctions between concepts associated with social justice. As I planned the activity, I developed a long list of words associated with social justice upon which to center the discussion. A critical friend called me out on this inconsistency, asking why I prescribed the words rather than asking the students to come up with their own. In response to this critique, I decided that instead of organizing the exercise around my own associations of social justice, I would begin by asking the students to construct a list of their values and associations connected to the topic. From there, we explored not just my own concepts but also the group's ideas and associations.

While this may seem small, the implications rippled out into the level of ownership the students had in the research process and, subsequently, their learning. I realized that shifting the way I viewed the students simultaneously changed how I engaged them and how they viewed themselves. I needed to develop an appropriate level of humility, remembering that I was learning alongside my students, that I didn't have all of the answers, and that they had just as much to teach me as I them.

Considering how I viewed my students was essential to my work of navigating my multiple roles in the research. This was about remembering that I was the researcher *and* a participant, an instructor *and* a learner. When I was connected to myself as participant and learner, I saw my students as collaborators and the sharing came naturally.

In all of this, it was also evident that I needed to be careful about the way that I held my roles of researcher and instructor, which led to the final question.

HOW AM I CARRYING MY AUTHORITY?

Even as I began to break down my notions of power, I required careful and daily attention to how I carried myself given the formal position I held at the university. The story I told in the beginning of the chapter of jumping up to the board to draw is a perfect example of this. While there may be instances when using a "teacher voice" is indeed beneficial, I became aware throughout my research of how frequently I go to that place without intention. Thus, being mindful of my use and exertion of power became a significant growth area for me. While it is easy, and even natural, for me to rely on a traditional lecturer-student approach, the most significant learning occurred when I stepped back, posed a question, or allowed students to engage more fully with one another. In a focus group in our final cycle of the research, one student offered,

> I noticed a shift in your leadership this year compared to last where ... it was just, um, less of a "Let's go to Stacey to tell us what to do." You stopped talking as much, which was weird for me because I was so used to hearing your voice. And when it was less present, I noticed it, but it allowed for a lot more growth and sharing of ideas amongst us. It helped to put us on the same level so we were able to draw from our own experiences and wisdom.

Just as this student suggested, as our research progressed, the students increasingly took on responsibility for the work. The most notable shift towards this was the cycle where we collectively analyzed the data, as students saw themselves as authors of the research. Similarly, the student's insistence that the process of analyzing our data was shared indicated a shift in how she viewed herself and her role in the research. Additionally, a few students later carried out their own research projects on the Women's Center, building on the work that we shared in the action research. In all of this, the implications for how I used my position, and what room that created for students to step into their own authority, was noticeable.

CONCLUSION

As the chapter title notes, this is about *power*. As action research seeks to bridge the researcher-practitioner divide, so too must we seek to bridge (or burn) hierarchical notions of teacher-student, leader-follower, you-me. Thus, my design asked me to move from a practice of power hoarding to one of power sharing, inviting students into the research process and roles of knowledge holder and creator. As a supervisor, advisor, and instructor to most of the participants in the research, a subquestion became: How do I engage my students as full contributors to—and authors of—the research, and their learning? Noticing power became the most prominent theme in my personal reflection and growth as a practitioner. I needed to consistently attend to the questions of how I was sharing, thinking about my students, and holding my authority.

An Aboriginal activist group from Queensland in the 1970s said, "If you have come to help me, you are wasting your time, but if you have come because your liberation is bound up in mine, then let us work together." At the Women's Center, we used this quote in our first cycle to think about how we understood our role in the pursuit of a socially just world. The message paralleled how I needed to shift my understanding of my role at the center; as an advisor, I was not there to "help" students figure something out that I already "got." Instead, we were co-explorers, with our learning and growth inextricably bound. I needed to view my students as knowledge holders, and frame the research in a way that honored that role and voice.

Opening up my concepts of who holds, controls, and defines knowledge not only informed how I engage in social justice education, but also transformed my advising and teaching philosophy as a whole. Now, in advising sessions and courses, I ask students where they want to go and what they want to learn and experience in our time together (sharing); I inquire about their experiences, stories, and knowledge (concept of students); and I am thoughtful about how I use my voice and position (carrying my authority).

I experienced a beautiful moment with a colleague recently that illustrated my learning and growth throughout my research and reflection. A fellow student in my class said something I found offensive and, as I felt pulled to interject, I instead posed a question. I inquired, not to correct, but to serve learning—his and my own—to see the perspective of another, and to seek to understand. It is through this lens that I now strive to serve as a teacher and advisor—not with answers, but with curiosity, humility, and a desire to facilitate a shared learning process.

WORKS CITED

Freire, P. (2000). *Pedagogy of the oppressed* (30th anniversary ed.). New York: Continuum.

SECTION FOUR

Trusting THE Process

> A journey of a thousand miles begins with a single step.
>
> —LAO-TZU (604–531 BC)

A good friend has this famous quote from Chinese philosopher Lao-tzu pinned over her kitchen sink. She says it reminds her to be calm, take things at a steady pace, and not get overwhelmed. For me, it just raises more questions. In which direction should I step? How do I know I'm going in the right direction? What happens if I want to change directions after I take that first step?

Getting started with action research can be similarly unnerving. When we initially begin to explore the questions that will guide our action research, there appear to be so many possibilities. We may fear that if we choose the "wrong" one, our entire action research process will fail. Questions will remain unanswered. Goals will go unmet. If this is where you find yourself, you are not alone. Over the years, we've worked with many educators who have felt similarly overwhelmed—and we've felt this way ourselves at times.

The good news is that the recursive nature of action research means that if you step in the "wrong" direction initially, you can always make changes as you go. The ship will right itself if you trust the sails—in this case, the internal voice reminding you what matters most, and the voices of your students and trusted colleagues. Some of the most successful action research experiences start from questions that are a bit wobbly at first, but are born out of an authentic desire to explore, learn, and grow. Many teacher researchers adjust their questions and adapt their methods as they learn more about their area of focus and receive feedback from their students.

In this way, good action research is much like good teaching. Both require high levels of responsiveness, and a willingness to bend to the needs of the students in our care. Yet, for many of us accustomed to thinking of research as a linear process, embracing the iterative nature of AR can be a difficult process in itself. How do we persevere through the challenges that are bound to arise? How do we stay committed to our path, but open to the possibilities we had not anticipated?

In the following chapters, teacher researchers tackle these questions, describing the challenges and rewards of engaging in action research and offering sage advice about how to stay calm through the journey.

Sam Gladwell, Laura McNaughton, and Melissa King each discuss the ways the action research process challenged them to let go of doing things the "right" way and instead, to embrace research as a dynamic process full of unexpected twists and turns. Sam shares how a bump in the road helped her to change her research question and methods midway through her research, reinvigorating her passion for the work. Laura reflects on how a seemingly "failed" action research project taught her to be open to unexpected answers and to let go of her own assumptions. Melissa describes how one cycle of action research leads to another, and how she learned to see the research process as more about "possibility than predetermined ideas."

Janet Ilko discusses how the structure of action research helped her explore an innovative teaching method—blogging with English Language Learners—and make a compelling case to colleagues for its value. As she systematically collected and analyzed her data, she developed ways to scaffold the blogging process for her students so that they were able to stick with it and embrace doing work that matters for authentic audiences.

Linnea Rademaker, Catherine Henry, and Laurel Gustafson reflect on the power of collaborative action research, specifically how having colleagues to reflect with—about the research process and what they were finding—helped them dig deeper into their analysis and discover unexpected findings that were central to their goals for students.

Finally, Daisy Sharrock discusses how her goals for students drove her evolving research design and kept her sane, even while the action research process wreaked havoc with her goal-oriented nature. She reflects on lessons learned about data collection and analysis, and how her own research came to life when she let go of the need to "prove something important" and instead looked closely at the themes emerging from her own data.

Questions to ponder as you read these chapters and think about your own work:

- What assumptions do you bring to your research? Are there particular findings or stories you were hoping to tell when you began? How do these compare with what you are finding now?

- How are you feeling about your research? If you are feeling stuck, how might you "unstick" yourself?
- What does it mean to you to explore something vs. prove something? How would you proceed in each case?
- What is a recent highlight from your research? How can you build on the momentum from this moment?
- How is what you are learning informing your next steps—both in data collection/analysis and in actions?
- Who can you invite to join you on your journey to help you analyze your data, unpack what it means, and reflect on the process?
- T. S. Eliot wrote, "We shall not cease from exploration, and the end of all our exploring will be to arrive where we started and know the place for the first time." Knowing that your research may take you in different directions than you had anticipated, where do you want to arrive? What do you want to understand more deeply when you get there? In other words, what is at the "core" of your research?
- How can you stay mindful of this "core" while remaining flexible and responsive to what emerges?

CHAPTER NINETEEN

Embracing Disequilibrium

SAM GLADWELL

At the beginning of the research process, I had to choose a question that would become the foundation of a full school year's worth of decisions, actions, and reflections. At the time, I felt an immense pressure to come up with the one, "right" question, a question that would sustain my interest and motivation over the long term. I felt like picking the right question was a test I had to pass in order to move on to the next phase of the research. I was determined not to be one of the people who had to change their focus later on; those people, I believed, had failed the test, had not thought things through, did not plan ahead, and as a result, had to pay the price for their mistakes with frustration and more work. I would not be one of those people.

When designing my question, I thought about what I wanted to get out of the research experience. More than anything, I wanted this experience to help me become a better teacher, and since I spent most of my time teaching math, it felt appropriate to center my question on math as well. Next, I thought about the different strategies I'd used as a teacher, the goals I had for my students, and the challenges I'd experienced with teaching math. Reflecting on these three factors helped me focus my question on math stations, a strategy I believed in yet had struggled with implementing the year before. After identifying the strategy on which to focus my research, I also wanted to name the desired end goal. What did I want my students to get from participating in stations? For me, the answer was clear: I wanted them to become effective problem solvers. That was it, two decisions made, and a question was born: "How can I use elementary math learning stations to differentiate instruction and increase student math proficiency?" At that point, I felt good about where I was heading in my research.

Fast forward to the beginning of the new school year. I had my question, I had some background knowledge, and I had a plan. However, something was missing, and addressing that "something" would ultimately mark a huge turning point in my research. It had to do with my goal of helping students become better problem solvers. I didn't know how to reliably measure a student's problem-solving ability, and if I couldn't take a baseline measurement, how could I determine whether learning stations increased this ability? I kept reading, reflecting, and searching, and just couldn't come up with a solution for this problem. I desperately needed to start collecting data, so I implemented my learning stations without the baseline measurement. With each day that went by, it felt like the potential validity of my findings was slipping away, along with the confidence I had in my question. My frustration led to a significant decrease in my motivation to engage in the research process, and that's when I realized I had a decision to make. I could either stubbornly cling to my beliefs about the one "right" question, or I could change my question to better reflect what I was excited to write about, which was my students' actual experiences with the stations.

I decided to seek feedback on my dilemma from graduate school colleagues. I described the situation to them, discussed what I was finding in the classroom, and presented some options for new research questions. With their support and guidance, I changed my question from "How can I use elementary math learning stations to differentiate instruction and increase student math proficiency?" to "What happens when I use student choice to differentiate instruction in elementary math learning stations?" That same night, I also learned a pretty important lesson: Change can be necessary and good, and the fear of making a mistake should not take precedence over listening to your intuition. From that point on, I stopped trying to do everything the "right" way and started embracing research as a dynamic process instead of a lockstep sequence of events. My renewed sense of enthusiasm for moving forward told me I had made the right decision.

ON PLANNING ...

My research question is not the only thing that changed over the course of the year. I also ended up scaling back my list of data collection methods, and perhaps most notably, I changed my plan for what stations would look like in my classroom. I wanted to let go of the tight control I had maintained over the stations during the previous year (when they hadn't gone well). In hindsight, though, I think that in my quest to let go I ended up letting go a little bit too much. On one hand, delegating much of the decision-making responsibility to the students taught me a lot about the power of student choice. On the other hand, because the stations were so well received and seemed to practically run themselves, I felt less compelled to keep them fresh and new, which I think probably diminished their educational value and the students' overall enjoyment of them. Ultimately, because the stations no longer required an enormous amount of maintenance, I ended up getting a bit lazy when it came to their upkeep. In the future, I am committed to maximizing their potential as an instructional strategy by updating the station offerings more frequently. Furthermore, while I believe that stations time could have been a worthwhile opportunity to pull kids together for targeted small group instruction, I highly valued the instances of "teachable moments" I experienced by not locking myself into a station or a small group and being able to freely move about the room. In the future I will try to maintain the ability to "float" and check in with all students, while occasionally using that time to pull together small groups as the need presents itself.

The action research process resulted in several positive outcomes for me as an educator, but stepping into the teacher-researcher role was not without its challenges. Personally, just getting started was difficult. I so badly wanted for everything to be "perfect" from the beginning, but the pressure of perfection actually ended up rendering me motionless for a long time. My advice to other researchers in this position is to just jump in and trust that you will learn everything you need to know along the way (as I had to do the first time I implemented stations!). Once I gave up the notion that "perfect" research conditions were attainable in my classroom and just went for it, everything fell right into place.

Another major challenge I faced was opening up my narrow definition of research to encompass the power of action research. Instead of spending hours reading piles of books and reporting on what other people have found, action research puts you right in the middle of the action, and that took some getting used to. My original research question reflected my limited view of research in that it tried to force a link between an instructional practice and a student outcome. If I had stuck with that original question, I would have missed out on telling the story I really wanted to tell, and the work would not have been nearly as meaningful to me or as transformative for my practice. Luckily, action research allows for flexibility and puts the researcher in control. All I had to do was listen to my intuition and give myself permission to make changes along the way to end up with a story I'm excited to share with others. I couldn't be happier that I ended up making those changes.

ON DATA ...

In the area of data collection, I ultimately decided to not use interviews very often during my research, and looking back, I believe that I may have missed out on a rich source of information. My hesitance to use interviews stemmed primarily from uncertainly about whom to interview, what to ask, when to conduct the interview, and how to manage the data. I was fortunate enough to get some insight on these issues from a fellow graduate school colleague who came in to conduct an observation, but unfortunately this experience happened near the end of the research cycle when it was just too late to implement a new method of data collection.

Although I missed out on using interviews as a data source, I found great success with two other methods of data collection that I have continued to use. The first tool is surveys. I have used beginning-of-the-year and end-of-project surveys in previous years with success, and as a result of my research, I expanded their usage to gather information about anything from how students are experiencing a particular activity to their thoughts about homework. The other data collection method I keep using is exit cards—index cards with a couple of questions for students to respond to so they can demonstrate their understanding or offer me feedback. Not only did the exit cards provide quantitative and qualitative data for my research, but they also functioned as a terrific method of student accountability. Both of these methods continue to be helpful in determining how to better differentiate instruction, much as they did during the research process.

Engaging in action research also opened my eyes to the benefits of using both qualitative and quantitative data to analyze student outcomes and behaviors. Before my research, I had often relied just on quantitative data (e.g., test scores, number of particular answers to a survey question) to interpret how my students were doing, but in doing so I was missing out on the richness of their own carefully selected words, thoughtful explanations, and creative ideas and wonderings. My research helped me to bring these two kinds of data together whenever possible to build a better understanding of my students.

Organization is key when collecting data in the classroom setting, whether those data represent one student or 100 students. Initially, I did not do a very good job of organizing my surveys and exit cards, which led to some unnecessary stress when I began to write up my findings. Having at least a preliminary plan for where to house the information, how to analyze it, and how to report it goes a long way in helping to maximize the value of the data and make all the time spent collecting the data worthwhile.

ON TRUST, STICKING WITH IT AND LETTING GO ...

Completing my research made a deep impact on my thoughts and actions as a teacher, and integrating student choice into my math learning stations led to outcomes I never could have imagined at the outset of the research process. One big lesson I learned was to trust the decision-making ability of my students. They demonstrated every week that when given the opportunity to choose their own working conditions, they became happier, more productive individuals, which was a wonderful thing to observe as their teacher. I will never go back to making all of the decisions for my students. I will also continue to promote a student-centered learning environment by embracing the creative ideas that will inevitably spring from their minds as they did during my research.

Finally, one more major take-away I had as a result of the research process was learning to not give up on an instructional strategy if it flops the first time around. In the past when a lesson didn't work or a method I was using in the classroom was hitting a roadblock, I abandoned it completely. Learning stations came dangerously close to meeting that same fate, and might not have been implemented in my class again had I not already committed to making them the focus of my action research. Despite some initial hiccups with getting the stations up and running, and modifying them to avoid the challenges I'd faced with them previously, I am so glad I stuck to it and was able to turn them into something meaningful and enjoyable for the students, and into something manageable for me. I am proud that I persevered through this challenge, and I have the research process to thank for giving me the confidence to go back and rework something that just wasn't quite right yet. This confidence has transferred over to other areas of my practice and helped me continue to grow as a teacher and as a person as well.

Ideas about letting go of control and being flexible were some of my most significant lessons learned through my research. Letting go of my original question rekindled my passion for the research process. Letting go of my previous approach to stations opened the door to a strategy that worked much better both for the students and for me. Letting go of my need for perfection allowed me to learn and grow more than I ever thought possible. These lessons have left a lasting impact on me both personally and professionally. Ironically, I set out to make my research benefit the students, but I had no idea how much I would end up getting out of it as well. I am excited to continue reaping the benefits of letting go and learning to trust in other areas throughout the rest of my life.

CHAPTER TWENTY

Letting Go

Heeding My Own Advice and Letting Go of Expectations

LAURA McNAUGHTON

With a deadline quickly approaching, I knew that I needed to come up with something and it needed to be quick. I had just spent 12 days in Peru with ten students attempting to conduct action research, and yet, I felt like nothing had come out of it. This whole process had started with the intent of answering a question. It took an entire semester to develop my question, a question that had to encompass my entire research, the perfect blend of theory, doubt, and curiosity. "How do I dialogue with students around social justice and privilege through a transformative learning experience like an international immersion trip?" I spent months writing it, and I created a strategy that would "answer" it. Yet, as I sat at my computer hoping the words would come, they evaded me. What did I learn in Peru? Did I do enough while in Peru to be able to answer this question? Or were the answers just different from what I was expecting?

Once the question was crafted, I developed an organized plan and timeline of what the research would look like: three cycles, with the trip incorporated as the second cycle. For the first cycle, I conducted three pretrip dialogues with the intent of inviting the students to be in community with one another, developing an understanding of what level each student was at developmentally in regards to their privilege and social justice, and creating a plan for the trip itself. The second cycle was an immersion trip to Peru. Throughout the trip, I was careful to take notes, to engage students in conversation during key moments, and to alter and tailor the nightly reflections based on the day's events and conversations. My third and final cycle was a reunion and closing dialogue. In this last dialogue, which was set up similarly to the three dialogues from the first cycle, I asked similar questions, and really was hoping to get certain answers.

With the research mostly done, a 12-day-long trip complete, and my action research chair anxiously awaiting a first draft, I started to reflect on whether or not I had actually answered my question. To my dismay, I realized that, even after all of my work, I was left with more questions than answers. I did it all right, I followed all the rules, and yet I still did not have the answers. With all these questions and a critical lack of answers, as an action researcher, how do I continue to analyze and make meaning of my data? How do I continue to reflect upon and be open to the learning that occurred?

As I started to reflect upon my research and consider these questions, I realized that with the recursive nature of action research, *failing can sometimes be more valuable than succeeding*. Sometimes I have to fail to realize what is needed the most. Sometimes you have to fail to do the learning. It took feeling like a failure to realize that my research question was not meant to be answered at all; instead, it was meant to guide me through the process, it was meant to break down the barriers I had put up for myself around my own learning, and it was meant to make me let go of the expectations I had developed for how and what my students would learn throughout this process.

All of the work leading up to the immersion trip was extremely valuable in the development of the Peru curriculum and program, but I failed to take into account one thing. The students were not as interested as I was in the issue of social justice, and I learned that their perspectives were very different from my own. I soon realized that things were not going to work out as I had originally "planned," and each student's experience or transformation as a result of the immersion trip was going to be different than the others, and they all were absolutely going to look different from my own transformative experiences. A valuable insight for me was learning that each individual looks at social justice differently, and how one understands elements of social justice greatly impacts their process of understanding and development, which then led me to realize that as an action researcher, I cannot predict the outcome of my research—I must be open to any of the answers my students provide, even the ones I am not expecting.

Throughout the 12-day trip, the students and I had influential experiences, the reflections were rich, and many amazing things were discussed during the dialogues, but somehow, throughout the trip, I felt like the students were not getting to where I thought they should be. During the three pretrip dialogues, all through the entirety of the trip, and after the trip, the group's mantra was "no expectations," and even with this mantra, I somehow could not heed my own advice, and I did have expectations for the students' experiences. I attempted to revise the questions for the dialogue, to challenge the students on new things, but I was not able to truly reflect until I returned. On reflection, I realized that my own past experiences were keeping me from allowing the space for the students' experiences to emerge. In the moment, I felt like the students needed to have a transformative experience, the same way I had been transformed on previous trips, but the experiences they were having were much different from my own.

Social justice is a complex and dynamic topic, and even knowing this, I still had the expectation that the students would be able to understand, articulate, and embody what social justice was and how it played out in their lives. As the trip continued, we had a reflection about privilege that was facilitated by my co-leader. It was toward the end of the trip, and there were a couple of students who were speaking up about unearned privilege being nonexistent. I was both mortified and dumbfounded. How was it possible that you just spent 10 days in a developing country and could not see privilege clear as day? I had failed; the trip was a bust, why did I bother?

Upon our return from the trip, after spending some time reflecting on the incident described above and other experiences, I felt like I had not improved my practice. I started questioning everything: Did I ask the right questions? Were the questions asked in appropriate order to come up with the kind of responses I was expecting, or were my expectations inappropriate? As I contemplated this possibility, I realized that some of the questions I had been asking myself that had emerged throughout the trip actually had answers, they were just not the answers I expected them to be. I thought I would see students willing to change their lives to make positive change—the same way I had felt. Instead of seeing an intensity of transformation, I saw my students start to think about privilege for the first time, I saw expressed in a group reflection a dissonance that they had never felt before. I witnessed the students self-authorize and see themselves in a new light, and I realize now how important self-authorship is for their development and capacity to have transformative experiences.

When my student started to speak up during that reflection about unearned privilege being nonexistent, I watched a student who had held back at many of the reflections speak to it; she owned her voice, she challenged the other student and provided examples of how privilege did exist. In Baxter Magolda's (2008) theory self-authorship is defined as "the internal capacity to define one's beliefs, identity, and social relations" (p. 269). In order to truly know oneself, one must be able to understand and explain to others their beliefs, values, and identity. Although initially I had not connected social justice to self-authorship, now it is clear to me that self-authorship is an important part of the process; in order to become socially conscious, people must have the capacity to define who they truly are and the values that are most significant to them. Throughout the trip, especially during reflections, I could see the moments when students stepped into the confident place where they were able to fully express themselves to the group and make meaning out of their experiences. And upon further reflection, I realized this meaning was often connected to both the students' own values and social justice.

Action research helped me understand that I did not need to get the answers I thought I needed to be successful. In fact, having data that did not fit my predetermined findings challenged me to go one step forward, to be open to unexpected answers, unexpected findings, to let go of the assumptions I had created around this experience. I had an incredible experience that was intentional and grounded in theory, and it resulted in my desire to become a better educator, teacher, and practitioner. I let go of expectations and created room for people's authentic experiences to emerge. The process of understanding and dialoging around social justice looked different than what I expected; the learning, the transformation, and the concept of social justice look different for every individual person.

In working with college students, I do not get to see the development of the student all the way through to the end. Students graduate, leave school, change departments, or move on. The most valuable and exciting part about action research is that even when the formal research is over, it never truly stops. I get to continue to ask myself the question I started with. This is the beauty of action research and why it fits so well with the work I do helping to develop and advise undergraduate students. I did not answer the question fully in the amount of time I had set out for research, but that does not mean I failed. If anything, I have provided myself with an array of additional questions, an understanding of how not to do my work, an idea of how I can continue in the future, and an understanding that the answers I am expecting to find are not always the answers I find.

I continue to learn from the research I had set out to complete within a specific amount of time. It is not just about what my students are learning, but also about what I'm learning. The lessons can sometimes be basic, such as, being flexible about making adjustments in expectations and digging deeper into a shared journey. My research question was not answered as precisely as I'd desired, and many more questions arose. However, I eventually realized that this provided assurance that a lot of learning took place—it just looked different than what I had expected.

For a student affairs professional like myself, action research is extremely valuable. Not just for me as a student, but for me as a lifelong learner, someone who wants to engage in my development and the development of my students. The research is now complete, but I know I will continue to learn and grow from the experience I had in embracing ambiguity, trusting the process, and allowing for new lessons and questions.

WORKS CITED

Baxter Magolda, M. B. (2008). Three elements of self-authorship. *Journal of College Student Development, 49*, 269–284.

CHAPTER TWENTY-ONE

Paradigm Shifts AND Possibilities

My Exodus from the Land of the Linear

MELISSA KING

I was given the formula for success, or so I thought, in kindergarten. It was my beloved teacher Mrs. Davis who taught me to color between the lines, churn butter, hatch baby chicks, and connect the dots to create fanciful creatures such as dolphins and dragons. All I had to do was follow the formula. Looking back, it was all quite linear. We learned our numbers in their prescribed order, the alphabet from A to Z, and the colors of the rainbow using that nifty little "ROY G. BIV" acronym. There was little room for interpretation, or error, for that matter. Everything had a beginning and an end, a start and a finish, and finite points in between. It was a road map easily followed. And this is how I learned to function within the classroom.

This linear formula seemed to be a recurrent theme throughout my elementary years. But one day, the formula didn't work. I was an experienced educator who had traversed many environments, but my K–12, even my undergraduate experiences never prepared me for the paradigm shift I would encounter by allowing the process of action research to take its course.

At the time, I was working in a nonpublic school that specialized in educating children on the autistic spectrum with significant behavioral challenges, and participating in the process of sending one of our students to a new, more restrictive placement. I was a member of the student's Individualized Education Plan team, which was charged with developing a plan to assist the student in accessing the curriculum. This particular case was wrought with dissension between the parents, school district, and my school. It would ultimately amount to the family requesting a due process hearing, which is an option parents can use to challenge their child's Individualized Education Plan. In the course of preparing for the due process hearing, I realized that we had a lot of information on the student, but it just didn't come together in a way that we could interpret it and make good decisions for the student. We were collecting data, but we weren't purposeful about the data collection.

I knew at that moment that if we were going to be accountable and responsible educators for this unique population of kids, we had to do better. Good intentions just weren't going to cut it. Data collection in my school was paramount. We were supposed to be using our data to drive decision making and to develop Individualized Education Plans for students with special needs. It could mean the difference between a child succeeding and failing. It also carried such significant legal implications that we were putting everyone at risk by not being clear about data collection. There was an obvious problem to solve. My plan became revamping and refining our data collection procedures.

I determined that the best resolve for this would be to take a participatory action research approach. I had read the literature, been given amazing insight and instruction from a professor skilled in the approach, and had an environment that was conducive to conducting research. I thought that we would document what we were doing, implement any necessary changes, and move forward to solid practices in data collection. That was my plan. We were going to do A, B, and C. Period. Talk to the teachers, find out what they do, decide what we were going to different, and then do it. Just like Mrs. Davis taught me. But it didn't quite turn out like that. The more we talked, the more I realized that my plan was not going to be neat and orderly.

FINDING OUT WHAT WE DO

Our initial purpose was to better understand our current data collection practices and use this new understanding to transform those practices to be more meaningful and collaborative. We began with three research questions: What are the current guidelines and/or requirements for the collection of data? What strategies are used to analyze data after it has been collected? How is data used to inform decision making after it has been collected and analyzed?

These three questions generated a great deal of raw data. It was like a scavenger hunt! Teachers began to tell their stories and communicate about their practices. We asked questions of ourselves and each other. What are we doing? How do we do it? Why do we do it? These initial conversations confirmed that our existing data collection practices were hit or miss at best. We had reduced ourselves to making tally marks on data sheets and estimates of when we thought a behavior had occurred.

The data collection was an event that happened at the close of the school day when teachers went back to the data sheets and filled in what they could recall of the day's events, child by child. We weren't collecting data in real time, we were lax in determining what data we were going to collect, and each staff member was interpreting behavior in a different manner. Everyone had a different perspective on "aggressive behavior," or a student being "off-task" or even "noncompliant."

Additionally, we discovered that the documents we were using weren't helpful and were quite time consuming. As a result, most teachers had devised their own "data collection systems"; some teachers were using time sampling as a strategy, some were taking interval data, some teachers were collecting data on all students every day, and some teachers were collecting data on only the most behaviorally challenged students. Finally, we discovered that all of this data remained in the form it was originally collected in. It was not charted, graphed, or translated into a form that could be presented to parents or easily discussed in the context of a team meeting. Unless there was some sort of records request or litigation, data was not thoroughly analyzed.

This initial step informed us about the numerous flaws in our data collection process and the lack of clarity in the program overall. Through conversations and sharing about data collection practices, it became clear to us that there was a lack of clarity in other aspects of the program as well, such as our communication with parents, expectations for students, and expectations for staff.

I had no idea what I was going to do. It seemed as if I had opened up a slew of issues that I was not prepared to deal with. I wanted this research project to be neat and tidy. I expected to have a shiny new pamphlet of procedures on data collection that all staff members would adhere to. I hadn't realized that there was so much diversity in teacher practices, not just in data collection but in how we addressed student behavior more generally. I began this process focused on improving our systems for collecting data, but now it looked like we might need to revamp our entire behavior modification program. I had to stop, and start again.

THE REBOOT: GOING BROADER

This was the very uncomfortable moment in my action research when I realized this was not as linear or finite a process as I thought it would be. It was a complete paradigm shift. I moved from the position of "Every project has a beginning and an end, and I know exactly what those points are in between" to realizations such as "Look at the possibilities," "I'm okay!" and "This is the epitome of research—to discover the truth, whatever that may be."

So I regrouped. I looked at my efforts to understand our data collection systems as one cycle of many. I didn't abandon the rich information I had collected.

I used it to inform my next cycle. And clearly, there was going to be a next cycle. I stayed the course and remained committed to the process. I realized that our new cycle would be about understanding the strengths and weaknesses of our existing program as a whole. We went back to the approach we used in cycle one, which was to develop research questions around our proposed issue or point of interest. In this cycle, we asked ourselves what our existing program practices encompassed. What do we believe? What do we actually subscribe to? What are our everyday practices? Again, we fact gathered as colleagues. We looked at schedules, routines, curriculum, reinforcement systems, and reward systems. We talked with teachers, instructional aides, occupational therapists, speech and language pathologists, behavior interventionists, educational therapists, and licensed clinical social workers and psychologists. We wound up with a potpourri of approaches, strategies, and practices that were being used within one program. Teachers had taken the original loose components of the program and were interpreting them in ways that worked for them. There was a great deal of variance, to say the least.

I had assumed once again that this cycle would give me all of the answers I would need to arrive at an end point, a clear solution. Again, my thought process was being challenged. I had accepted the turn of events in the first cycle but suddenly realized it was not some sort of anomaly. This is action research. This was not the end. But from here, it did begin to narrow.

Our second cycle had highlighted a need to improve the existing behavior modification program for children in our school who exhibited high-risk behaviors such as physical aggression towards peers and staff, property destruction, and self-injurious behaviors, as well as lower-risk behaviors related to social skills deficits, depression, distractibility, extreme rigidity, perseveration, and noncompliance. We embarked on a third cycle.

Our research questions sought to understand the types of behavior intervention methods or approaches staff members used in real time within the school setting, and how a school might structure a comprehensive behavioral intervention program manual (and what type of information it might include). Our effort to answer these questions involved gathering and reviewing program artifacts, developing teacher and staff surveys, and observing school staff. We surveyed teachers and instructional aides regarding their perspectives on what their roles were in the classroom. We asked them about how they respond to children exhibiting behavior challenges throughout the day and what tools and strategies they use to help reduce or extinguish the behaviors of the students in their care. As you can imagine, this generated a whole new wealth of information that gave us insight into ourselves.

We also explored national and international programs that support a similar demographic of children to identify potential best practices. We scoured search engines such as ERIC and EBSCOHOST searching for articles on best practices in behavior management for children with special needs. We read articles, journals, reports, and studies. We created a spreadsheet of what we had discovered.

We felt that this, surely, would be the end of the road. But it certainly was not. As we pored over our pretty spreadsheet and looked at all of the wonderful, powerful approaches being used around the country and the world to modify behavior, we realized that we didn't know where our program fit in. However, we also discovered that there were about ten common best practices that supported students with behavioral challenges in the classroom setting. There must be a positive relationship between home and school, positive relationships between colleagues, and most definitely, a positive relationship with students. Additionally, the way the classroom furniture is organized is important, as are modifying their curriculum when needed, social skills instruction, data collection, data analysis, positive reinforcement, and an appropriate staff-to-student ratio.

What we found was that we were, in fact, doing all of those things. Some needed a bit more polishing and attention than others, but they were all occurring in our environment. This provided us with a wonderful starting point. Through all of our previous cycles, we had come to understand our own program better. We now knew what areas needed to be adjusted, and how important it was to communicate the aspects of a program, and the common expectations, in a manner that is clear for both students and staff. We had arrived at the point of refining our existing practices to ensure that we were delivering the best academic, social, and behavioral program possible.

The end result was a period filled with implementation. We were able to accomplish amazing things by being open to the process. My ability to move outside of the lines and open myself up to pursuing the truth made the difference. Once I became familiar with the potential for action research to evolve, the real layers unfolded into marvelous benefits to our students, staff, and overall program. We were even able to revisit our data collection systems and make improvements. It happened a few cycles down the road, but it did happen! And I left this adventure understanding the value of all that Mrs. Davis had taught me, but also armed with the knowledge that action research is a recursive process. It can be more circular than linear, and more about possibility than predetermined ideas.

CHAPTER TWENTY-TWO

"Can't We Just Do A Worksheet?"

Persevering through Challenges When Implementing Action Research

JANET ILKO

When we are no longer able to change a situation—we are challenged to change ourselves.
—VICTOR E. FRANKL

I have always considered myself a writer. I have boxes of journals documenting teenage angst, college notes and papers, and scrapbooks documenting family life. When I became a teacher I wanted to share my passion for writing with my middle school students, many of whom are English Language Learners. I wanted to help them find their voices and learn to communicate effectively so that they could advance academically and professionally and advocate for themselves and their communities. But as the years went by, I found that this goal was increasingly stymied as more and more time was dedicated to preparing for end-of-the-year standardized tests. I blogged about my frustration at the end of the school year in 2012:

> I am mad that so much of the past month has been spent testing, or talking about "THE TEST" or prepping for the test, or doing make ups, and we have lost our way ... I know the results do not solely measure our progress. [The test] measures only that you have or do not have stamina to test for that incredible amount of time. It doesn't measure writing in any real sense, your oral language skills, or our sense of identity or community ... I need to find better ways that document your learning throughout the year that will show your growth as writers, in grammar, in voice, in content. I want a portfolio of real student work that can stand up to the bubble data that is currently being used to measure progress in a neat, tidy, if in my opinion, somewhat inaccurate or at least isolated view of who your are as a learner and we are as a writing community. (Ilko, 2012)

From this post came the realization that I needed to do something different the following year, unless I wanted to be sitting in June feeling the exact same frustration. As a recent convert to blogging, I'd seen the power of online writing in my own life, and wondered if it could have a positive impact on my students. How might they respond to having an online audience? How could digital writing facilitate communication and collaboration among the class? Could this authentic form of 21st-century communication mitigate the stilted approach to writing that the test demanded? I knew that if I was going to move in a new direction, I would need to be prepared to justify the instructional changes to my principal, my students, their parents, and myself, so I decided to build an action research inquiry around this work in order to more systematically assess students' learning and adjust my instruction in response to these assessments. I formed this research question: "Would creating a student-generated digital space and blog improve the writing of my English Learners?"

A SUMMER TO EXPLORE: FOCUSING THE LITERATURE REVIEW

I spent my summer vacation learning everything I could about blogging with students. I discovered that there was limited research on using student-generated digital spaces with Long-Term English Learners. In late June 2012, I attended the conference of the International Society for Technology in Education (ISTE). With a laser focus, I went to every session or talk on what it meant to blog with students. I asked for advice from professional bloggers and fellow teachers on start-up ideas for blogging, and compared platforms. I then continued my lit review on student blogging and digital portfolios. As the summer wore on, I discovered the simple truth: There was no magic digital space that worked for every situation.

In mid-July I continued the exploration alongside students in the San Diego Area Writing Project's Writing for Change Academy. Each summer, the project brings students together for a 2-week program to inspire student voice through digital writing (http://www.writingforchange.net). In summer 2014 we explored blogging with students, and we discovered the power of audience. We joined a group of young bloggers through a site called The North School Writers Club (http://thenorthschool.com/writersclub/). Even in that short period of time, we saw a glimmer of something interesting: Students wrote not just for themselves or their writing coach, but to inform a larger audience and participate actively on the site. Students were not only producing their own work, but also responding to the work of others. They wanted to read and respond to their peers' postings almost as much as they wanted to create their own messages. My enthusiasm grew, and

I decided to weave this platform into my class in the fall. The program would be based on these three ideas:

(1) Student choice inspires voice,
(2) Students need to be producers, not consumers of digital media, and
(3) Documenting and evaluating this work as a teacher and as the writer in these digital spaces has value.

CREATING THE SPACE: FINDING A PLACE FOR AUTHENTIC EXPRESSION

Fast-forward to the beginning of the school year, to our writing classroom. I have three classes of 7th and 8th grade English Learner (EL) students, with an average of 32 students in each class. These students have been selected to be in my class because they struggle with content area reading and writing. Many of my students also have motivational issues due to their lack of language development progress. They had experienced persistent low levels of success every year in a public school system that promotes English-only pedagogical practices with teachers who often feel unprepared and unsupported in working with the varied and deeply complex nuances of multiple language systems within a mainstream classroom setting. I thought that using this new student-generated blogging platform would be the answer. Was it? The results indicate a resounding "Yes!"—and sometimes, an equally resounding "No!"

The idea of creating individual blogs at first felt overwhelming, and it was a struggle to take those first steps. Many of the initial challenges were logistical. I had to find a platform that would work for this project, given that these were middle schoolers who were relatively new to technology. I had to find something that was relatively user-friendly, with enough tech features to promote students becoming true producers of their own digital content. The final hurdle was to alleviate the concerns of both our school administration and our parent community, who needed assurance that the students would be both productive and safe in this new digital environment. We had permission slips for everything. As a teacher, I knew that these logistical considerations were crucial to our instructional success, but as an action researcher who wanted to focus, I found myself impatient. I wanted to focus on the work with students, to collect data to see how they would respond pedagogically, and to determine the overall impact on their learning. Jumping through these administrative hoops made me feel at times that the project focused too much on these challenging details and too little on the potential achievements of my students.

NOW THE REAL WORK BEGINS

As new bloggers, we spent about a month learning about digital citizenship, cyber safety, and the purpose of a blog. We used lessons from Common Sense Media (http://www.commonsensemedia.org) to provide information to both students and families. We began with paper blogs, creating our spaces and topics and learning how to post academic vs. social comments. Students were initially excited about the project, and were eager to design their space. Then came the first few posts, and the secret was out—digital writing was still work! Although they had freedom in topic selection, there were still required writing genres we needed to cover. Some students became less than enthusiastic once the space was created, and about 2 months into the project there was an outcry from more than a few students: "Can't we just do a worksheet?" I was stunned. Here I thought I had solved the problems of the educational world. My students would embrace independent reading and writing because it was on a topic of their choosing. They would be self-motivated to select articles of interest, read for purpose and enjoyment, and support their views in our research projects, and we would go on our merry way as a cyber community with academic discourse flying through our comment pages. I quickly discovered that we would need a tremendous amount of underlying structure to create blog spaces that were academic as well as personal for my students.

Structure came from my determination to view this project not just as a teacher, but also as an action researcher. Rather than throwing in the towel, I went back to the literature I reviewed over the summer. I reconnected with other teachers who were blogging with students, and recognized that this was not an all-or-nothing endeavor. By keeping my action research perspective, I had a lens that allowed me to push through the logistical challenges with a focus on the impact on student learning, and that kept me moving forward step by step.

Blogging is not an easy endeavor. With student choice comes the challenge of student focus. When students asked, "Mrs. Ilko, can't we just do a worksheet?" it really was code for, "I'm frustrated, this is too hard." And so I pushed them, prodded them, begged, and sometimes (figuratively) stood on their heads to get something onto the page. Not every blog post sang off the screen, but that wasn't the goal. With blogging comes repeated writing, and combined with an audience, that has the potential to improve the content as well as writing fluency. We soon discovered that good writing, and hosting a blog site, required dedication, time, and effort.

We had other technical issues to contend with as well. The San Diego Kids Write site was not easy to navigate on our school platform. We had issues with getting in and out of the site. There were times when it took so long to download to enter the site that students wrote their pieces elsewhere and posted them later. We also discovered that Kidblog could not hold some of the larger digital movies or projects that were created, so I posted that work onto our classroom site or the Writing for Change site. It was awkward, but a compromise.

But the greatest challenge came in facing my own fears and demons. I began to question myself on a weekly basis. Did we take on too much this first year? Were my students learning to be better writers? Would they be prepared for the spring tests looming in the not so distant future? Was I ever going to spend a weekend not on the computer?

It would have been easy to give up and move back to the familiar, but we did not. Again, the action research lens helped to calm my fears and focus the work. With weekly reviews of student writing and a continual return to my research question, I was able to systematically navigate through the process. Maintaining an action research lens gave direction to what sometimes felt like one long, winding, and often unwieldy road trip through uncharted territories.

I also knew that in order to evaluate this project, I needed to consistently consult with the most important component of this project, my *students*. On multiple occasions, I asked, "Why do you blog? Do you think it is making you a better writer?" I wanted to ensure that every student had the opportunity to share their thoughts, not just those at either end of the spectrum of "love it or leave it." Although most of the responses were positive, I have to admit there were a few students who responded, "I blog because Mrs. Ilko makes me." Overall, I was pleasantly surprised (and grateful) that the majority of students said that they enjoyed the writing process, and they liked seeing what others had to say. Nancee shared, "Writing makes you feel good. Sometimes you don't have anyone to tell what you are feeling. Sometimes nobody understands you. When you write, it makes you feel better. When I first started writing, I didn't like it. But now, I really enjoy it." And Siobhann eloquently stated, "Why do I like blogging, you ask? Because people actually hear my voice and I let it be heard."

ASK, ANSWER, AND ASK AGAIN

Throughout this year I revisited my initial question often. "Would creating a student-generated digital space and blog improve the writing of my English Learners?" With every passing week, as the work continued, I asked these two additional questions: "Is this particular lesson or project creating a better reader or writer?" and "How will we know?"

Spring was looming, and I knew that soon, over a 3-week period, I would be giving standardized tests that would attempt to define my students as readers and writers. Coming full circle from that open letter to my students last spring, what I hoped to achieve was to provide an additional view into their growth as readers and writers.

I believe that students need to be producers, not just consumers, of digital media. To do that, I need to teach students not only to think critically about what they want to say, but also to be able to analyze those messages sent through digital media in their daily lives. By producing their own blog, students are forced to create a personal space. They make decisions about the media and words that bring their message clearly to their audience. It no longer is about how many cool pictures I can post, but about what those images bring to my blog to enhance my message. The purpose of a blog is to share your views with an audience. Students now reflect on what will bring someone to read their posts. If I want to build an audience, I also need to consider not only my own views, but also what will interest my readers. How can I clearly state my point of view and ideas and spark a discussion on my page? That sense of audience has taken our revision to a new level.

Setting up our blogs with categories has allowed my students to create a digital portfolio space. Hopefully, as they reflect over these last few weeks, they will be able to see the growth and changes in their writing. At the end of the year we won't be looking at just standardized testing data when evaluating our learning and academic growth. We will be able to see ourselves as writers, producers, and editors.

As the teacher, for me this time of reflection is new. I will spend the last week of school reflecting with my students, rather than scoring stacks of essays on my own. Their portfolios will include their voices, their reflections, and that makes this project worth the time and effort. When it comes to placing students in their classes next year, I won't be looking at a single number score; my 7th graders who come back to me next fall will have this digital space to which to return.

Blogging with my students isn't just a project or assignment; it is now a way of life in our classroom. Throughout the school year we have had numerous district office personnel, school board members, and community leaders visit our classroom to see the students' work. We participated in National Digital Learning Day and shared our work on academic commenting with teachers, politicians, and even Secretary of Education Arne Duncan, through our Edmodo feed. Our students are proud of what they have written and appreciate the larger audience of significant adults, but the real work began long after the visitors came and went. The work is in the day-to-day struggle in learning to be a digital writer.

It will take another 2 or 3 years to refine this practice, but I am confident that I will be able to continue to integrate digital writing into my classroom instruction because of the structure action research provides. Because I was investigating this work as an action researcher, I was able to view the work through multiple lenses. By evaluating the student work over time, adjusting our lessons to meet the needs based on data, and allowing time to reflect on the process, we created a structure of research and exploration that can be built upon year after year. We are in the early developmental stages; it is messy, and challenging and wonderful. I have more questions than answers, which is what I love about teaching young writers.

But I feel that by taking on the role of action researcher, I have the structure and confidence to continue to move this work forward. We grew as writers and learners in our classroom together. It is my hope that each of my students walks away from this experience not only able to improve their academic standing, but more importantly, feeling valued, and empowered to share their voice.

WORKS CITED

Cutts, M. (2011, March). Try something new for 30 days [Video file]. TED Talks. Retrieved from http://www.ted.com/talks/matt_cutts_try_something_new_for_30_days.html

Ilko, J. (2012, May 26). Dear room 207, coming back from the edge of the testing abyss [Web log message]. Retrieved from http://writinginmyhand.org/?p=491

Long-Term English Learners, California AB-21-93 (2011–2012). Retrieved from http://leginfo.legislature.ca.gov/faces/billNavClient.xhtml?bill_id=201120120AB2193

Blog sites referenced:

http://kidblog.com

http://thenorthschool.com/writersclub/

http://www.writingforchange.net

http://www.commonsensemedia.org

CHAPTER TWENTY-THREE

Hidden Gems

Finding Unanticipated Outcomes through Collaborative Action Research

LINNEA RADEMAKER, CATHERINE HENRY, AND LAUREL GUSTAFSON

On a warm afternoon toward the end of the school year, we sat down to look at the changes in student progress as measured over the course of the school year by standardized literacy assessments. This data was collected as part of the measurements chosen for an action research project to look at the effectiveness of a literacy program in improving struggling students' literacy skills. Most of the children we had been tracking (all of whom had Individual Education Plans, or IEPs) had made some progress, and a couple had made outstanding progress. Most were still reading below grade level, which was not unusual, as many of these students began the year far below grade level. But as we looked closely at the data, our conversation shifted from numbers and aggregate scores to individual stories. "This little girl has a severe learning disability due to a long-term illness," Cathy explained. "She has struggled with literacy and received failing grades since kindergarten. But over the course of this year, I've noticed a change. During this project she received her first 100% on a spelling test. Her self-esteem has improved and she has an improved attitude toward school. Her mom came up to me last week to tell me thank you for helping her daughter feel successful at school for the first time ever."

The story above is a small example of how reflection helped us uncover broader and deeper results from action research. The three of us—Linnea, a university professor of action research; Cathy, a special education teacher; and Laurel, a 2nd-grade classroom teacher—worked together over the course of a school year to complete an action research project to try and improve student literacy. We focused specifically on students with Individual Education Plans

(IEPs) who were mainstreamed in Laurel's classroom. Our work yielded multiple interesting findings, but one recurring theme in our conversations as we worked to analyze and report on the data was a discussion of the tangential results of collaborating on an action research project.

If we were to look strictly at the standardized test results as a single measure of the impact of our action research, we would likely be disappointed. These initial quantitative results did not reveal the spectacular literacy growth that we had wanted. But as we unpacked the stories behind those results, we found ourselves speaking of OTHER changes that had occurred in individual students, the parents, and the school.

As a university professor and occasional visitor to this 2nd grade classroom, Linnea was the first to recognize that these unexpected changes might be interesting, and began asking probing questions to encourage reflection on these events. Collaborative action research can change participants and increase communication and sharing of practice (Avgitidou, 2009), thereby increasing participant learning. Critical to this learning is the need to reflect on both the participation and processes of action research implementation. By taking the time to reflect on the entire process, and not just the test scores, we were able to uncover some unexpected improvements in the context and in the students. Below, we discuss a few examples of our "unexpected" findings.

REFLECTING ON CHANGES IN CONTEXT

Cathy: Over the years, I've noticed that students with IEPs engaged in spelling instruction in the regular education classroom would often be sitting pretending to be working while patiently waiting for me to arrive. When I arrived, I would have to lead them in their work, often "spoon-feeding" them the answers. Within a few months of beginning the new literacy program (which, as a side benefit, also fosters independent learning), I began to notice that the students with whom I worked were already absorbed in their individualized word-sort tasks before I arrived to work with them. Students still asked questions, but I noticed that the questions were more about "how" to proceed, rather than "what to write." Students were engaged in discovering the answers for themselves, instead of having me giving them the answers, as before. We were seeing student discovery leading to student mastery of literacy concepts at individualized, developmentally appropriate levels.

This finding was not in our original "research questions," but, was still important to note, as such activity can lead to improved learning, and may be an avenue for further action research in the future. As classroom teachers, both of us felt that the previous literacy program didn't leave much room for the necessary differentiation needed for the diverse learners in their classroom, and that this differentiation was the key to ongoing, long-term improvement for these students.

REFLECTION LEADS TO MORE QUESTIONS AND MORE DATA COLLECTION

Laurel: One area that we had concerns about was parents' perceptions of this differentiated literacy program. Parents would make casual comments throughout the year at varying times—some in support of the program, and some with concerns about their child's progress. I began to perceive that parents of high-achieving students were worried that their students were not being challenged. Instead of reacting at the moment and removing the high-achieving students from the program, we decided to survey the parents to determine what they really thought of the program. Nine out of the 25 families in my classroom responded to the survey (parents in two-parent households were counted as one), and they included parents of high-achieving, grade-level, and at-risk students. We found that they were overwhelmingly supportive of the program (all surveys were marked "4" or "5" on a 5-point Likert scale). Again and again, parents came up to us and said thank you for what we were doing. At the beginning of the year, when a few parents indicated they had reservations about the program, we were afraid that the school administration might become involved and suggest changes. However, through the use of a survey, we now had data to take to the administration showing parent support for the program.

REFLECTING ON CHANGES LEADS TO SELF-EMPOWERMENT AND UNEXPECTED OUTCOMES

Linnea: Continued participation in action research, particularly reflection, can assist researchers in looking towards the future, scanning for problems and trying out solutions, and always thinking of what can be done better, without having an outside agent dictate what should be examined (Eilks & Markic, 2011). During our conversations, Cathy and Laurel were able to reflect on the project while it was ongoing, leading to further cycles of data collection, and were able to reflect on it again afterwards to expand upon their perceptions of changes resulting from the action research project. This type of continuous cycle of reflective practice is empowering in that practitioners take responsibility for their contexts and practice, believing that continuous change is synonymous with continuous improvement.

Believing that such reflection can lead to new questions in their own contexts, Cathy and Laurel continued this project into the next year, with new children and new issues. Much of their enthusiasm centered on the differentiation that this program allowed. In this way, they noted that they were able to help students progress by beginning at each child's developmental level. What they didn't expect was that other teachers were watching, and that their project would have influence on the entire school. Teachers in their school building heard about what they were doing, and the administration asked Cathy and Laurel to present their work at a building-level teacher in-service, and, subsequently, at a district in-service. The next year, the teachers in the building had an option to adopt the new literacy program or to stay with their own work. Almost all of the teachers decided to adopt the new program.

The type of reflection we've written about in this chapter is what Mertler (2012) referred to as "Action Planning" (p. 208). Mertler noted how important it was to take time to personally reflect on the project and the larger scope of the project within the context. Mertler asserted, "It [continuous reflection, or Action Planning] provides opportunities for reflecting on where you have been, what you have learned, and where you are going from here" (p. 208). Van Manen (1995) suggested that reflection is "challenging," and although disciplined practice is required, one must also have an "attitude" of wanting to change or learn something new about oneself or one's context. Cathy and Laurel continued to exhibit the quality of wanting to change, and wanting to know more about how to improve their practice. The challenge is in the interwoven contexts in which we practice—the contexts of ourselves, our collaborators, the students and their parents, and the institution. Van Manen explained: "The thinking on or about the experience of [practice] and the thinking in the experience of [practice] seem to be differently structured. Retrospective reflection on (past) experiences differs importantly from anticipatory reflection on (future) experiences" (1995, p. 34). Cathy concurred, noting:

> I think as a teacher you're always self-reflecting; but if you're not taking the time to talk about it with someone else, the thoughts kind of "go by the wayside," and you don't do anything about it. If you take the time to reflect and share, then you focus on what needs to be done, and make a plan to do it.

WORKS CITED

Avgitidou, S. (2009). Participation, roles, and processes in a collaborative action research project: A reflexive account of the facilitator. *Educational Action Research, 17*(4), 585–600. doi:10.1080/09650790903309441

Eilks, I., & Markic, S. (2011). Effects of a long-term participatory action research project on science teachers' professional development. *Eurasia Journal of Mathematics, Science & Technology Education, 7*(3), 149–160.

Mertler, C. A. (2012). *Action research: Improving schools and empowering educators* (3rd ed.). Thousand Oaks, CA: Sage.

Van Manen, M. (1995). On the epistemology of reflective practice. *Teachers & Teaching, 1*(1), 33–50.

CHAPTER TWENTY-FOUR

Tackling THE Ambiguities OF Action Research

Advice for the Goal-Oriented Practitioner on How to Stay Sane

DAISY SHARROCK

"Would you tell me, please, which way I ought to go from here?"
"That depends a good deal on where you want to get to," said the Cat.
"I don't much care where—" said Alice.
"Then it doesn't matter which way you go," said the Cat.
"—so long as I get *somewhere*," Alice added as an explanation.
"Oh, you're sure to do that," said the Cat, "if you only walk long enough."

—LEWIS CARROLL, *ALICE IN WONDERLAND*

I do not fall asleep watching movies in bed. No matter how bad the movie is, or how late the hour, I will keep my eyes pried open with toothpicks until the closing credits. I am goal-oriented. Set a carrot in front of me and I will devise a way to eat it. This is a great trait for many things—studying for tests, writing a resume, driving to work—but not so great for large complex tasks that require simultaneously tracking multiple developing threads, threads that constantly double back on themselves and cross-link randomly. Tasks like action research.

Of course I didn't know this when I began, so let's back up. The directive was simple. Action research: Write a proposal about what you wish to explore, explore it, and then write up your findings. It appeared so easy! Which is why, I suppose, the murky quagmire that ensued took me completely by surprise. At first, I was crystal clear about my area of research: inquiry. I wanted to explore inquiry in the classroom. What did it look like? What were the best strategies? How did students experience it? Then I tried it. What I thought was going to unfurl like pearls on a string turned out to be a jumbled tangle of twine. I couldn't even find an end to start with!

REVELATION 1: IT'S OKAY TO LOOK AT YOUR GOAL THROUGH A NEW LENS

The realities of exploring any one idea in a classroom setting inevitably lead to a tangled web of confounding factors. Inquiry was hard. Students struggled significantly, and many shied away from the thinking that was involved. Some had prior exposure to asking their own questions. For others this was an entirely new concept. They had never been asked to ask questions before. How could I support these diverse learners? Finding resources was a challenge, and student motivation was dropping like a rock.

Suddenly, inquiry wasn't just inquiry anymore. It was a host of other related issues that sprang up like a dense thicket: prior exposure, challenging work, student motivation, scaffolding, authenticity, and family support networks. This was incredibly frustrating, because I knew what I *wanted* my classroom to look like: engaged students working on interesting questions they had posed, coming to "Aha!" moments, and rising to meet new challenges, but the reality seemed very distant from my utopian action research fantasies. As I tried to tease out inquiry from these other factors, I began to feel like I couldn't explore one without exploring them all. Which, of course, would be crazy. I needed to reestablish a manageable goal.

I slowly came to the understanding that, no matter how much I *wanted* to pursue all the issues I'd noticed in my classroom, to stay sane, I had to pick just one. After some thinking about which factor I felt the strongest about, I chose to look at student motivation *as it pertained to inquiry*. Inquiry was still my focus, but out of all the confounding factors, motivation felt like the most significant obstacle to successful classroom inquiry. I felt a little like I was at the optometrist. In my head I could hear Dr. Hall perfectly: "Is your action research goal clearer with this lens, or this one?" I tinkered with my original action research question, which focused on inquiry alone, and came up with a new question: How can I effectively scaffold inquiry learning in my classroom, and how does it affect student motivation?

By restructuring my research question to incorporate both inquiry and one of the major obstacles to its successful implementation, I managed to explore both while narrowing my research focus to a more manageable slice of my classroom environment. This did wonders to keep me on track when I began to analyze my data. If something didn't pertain to inquiry or motivation I could leave it alone for now; it was a thread to be picked up at a later date, after my current action research project was finished.

REVELATION 2: DON'T REINVENT THE WHEEL—BORROW IT INSTEAD

With a clear goal and my research question in hand, I realized I needed to collect some baseline data. This was intimidating for two reasons. The first was that truthfully, I didn't yet feel completely secure with my newly minted research question. What if it was still too big, too complex? What if I needed to refine it further? The second concern was that I had absolutely no idea how to collect baseline data that would still be relevant at the end of my action research. What are the important questions to ask my students, given that I have no idea where my question will lead me? And how on earth do I figure them out on my own?

I floundered for a while, caught in that nebulous quantum state of knowing that I had to develop some questions, but also knowing that I had no idea how to create them. Finally, I returned to the literature. Perhaps some other goal-oriented researcher had already created and vetted surveys that I could tweak to fit this situation. Lo and behold, I found exactly what I was looking for—a survey on grit by Angela Duckworth and Martin Seligman (2005), and a survey on intrinsic and extrinsic motivators for academic motivation by Robert J. Vallerand and colleagues (1992). I also used their surveys to come up with my own survey, assessing inquiry skill knowledge, and collected my baseline data. Searching online and in the literature for useful surveys or tools developed by other professionals turned out to be well worth the effort.

REVELATION 3: GO DEEP

Once I had accomplished my baseline data goal, I once again felt the queasy feeling of goal-lessness. Which direction do I choose now? Like Alice in the quote that heads this chapter, faced with an open-ended question to explore, I realized that I definitely wanted to get *somewhere*, and in order to do so, I better get cracking. I realized that the broad sweep of data I had collected from my students provided an overview of the class, but in order to find that elusive end in the tangle to start pulling, I needed more information. I needed *details*. I needed focus students. I selected six students, based on their initial survey results and my classroom observations, to interview both individually and as part of a panel. They represented a good cross-section of the class in terms of motivation and levels of inquiry experience.

Where surveys provided a whole-class snapshot of static parameters, much like an aerial photograph, interviews provided core samples. Being able to ask follow-up questions to delve deeper into student perceptions and experiences was extremely useful. These interviews provided a rich context in which to analyze motivation and inquiry. Underlying motivational factors that could have remained hidden, such as troubles at home or internal passions, were shared, and that provided a more nuanced understanding of student motivation for inquiry in the classroom. Interviews helped me identify key students who became case studies for my research. Their unique stories added depth and personalized the action research process.

REVELATION 4: GO BROAD (AGAIN)

In contrast to the intensely focused data that resulted from interviews, journaling provided an ongoing and excellent overall view of class perceptions and trends that also proved to be incredibly useful. I asked the students through journal prompts every question I could think of related to inquiry or motivation, and a number of interesting themes emerged. I discovered that while most teenagers list external motivating factors as the most significant factors behind accomplishing something challenging, some motivators were nobler than others. The student who claimed to want to do well in school in order to become a dentist and work in impoverished communities was certainly closer to intrinsic motivation than the student who studied only because his parents would take away his computer if he didn't. Making a distinction between types of external motivation resulted in a return to the literature and the discovery of earlier work that explored similar themes. It was as if one of the ends of the ball of twine had finally become exposed, and I could begin the journey of unraveling the snarl. Ever so slowly, the knot began to unravel, and my understanding of student motivation and how it related to inquiry began to deepen. Themes became clear and patterns emerged. New questions arose, and my class and I devised ways to explore them.

REVELATION 5: SURVEYS ARE NUMERICAL GOLD

To assess progress and collect numerical data, I collected student responses to a variety of survey questions over the semester. Along with the interview responses, surveys provided useful data regarding individual and class trends that brought up new questions. These new questions became new journal prompts for the whole class. And the cycle repeated itself.

Even though at the start I was worried about collecting baseline data on a question I wasn't quite ready to commit to, it proved to be a stroke of inadvertent genius. In those beginning few weeks, as my focus wavered between different themes to explore, it would have been easy to put off collecting baseline data until I felt sure about my chosen course of action. The truth is, I didn't feel truly secure about what I was exploring until *halfway through* my action research. At the end of the semester, I dusted off the original baseline survey and the students took it a second time. I was impressed that the questions were still valid, and the final survey data showed a significant shift compared to the original survey data. The results provided a perfect bookend.

REVELATION 6: SEEK TO EXPLORE, NOT TO PROVE

When I started my action research, one of the significant challenges I faced, as a goal-oriented individual, was the need to Prove Something Important with my research. I felt that research was about discovering something new, the "Eureka!" moment that I could share with the world. If I didn't Prove Something Important, then my research was a failure. Of course, my intellectual side knows this is poppycock, but my emotional side doesn't always listen to reason. This self-imposed goal was responsible for a fair amount of strife in the first month of my action research. I was so busy looking for Something Important that I was forgetting to spend time with the details, the subtle undercurrents of the class.

Finally, one Sunday after I had graphed survey data every which way I could think of (What do girls think? Boys? How does GPA figure in?), I stopped and reread a transcript from my first panel interview. I read it a couple times. Slowly, an interesting pattern emerged from the student responses. My lower-grit students tended to mention external motivating factors, while my high-grit students tended to mention internal motivating factors. It was only in a couple places, easy to miss if you weren't looking for it, and possibly nothing important at all, but it raised a question that I knew I had to follow up on. The next day, I had the students journal about motivating factors in order to follow the thread. Their responses led to a new classroom activity and a new survey. Which led to my new question, and before I knew it, I was immersed in my action research.

I realized that my focus needed to shift away from Proving Something Important towards exploring the trends I found in my data. I had to adapt my methods to explore questions as they presented themselves. By staying focused on the next interesting question, I managed to let go of the need to prove something, and my action research began to weave a tapestry of interlocking themes. The picture that emerged was far richer than a pat answer, and much more profound. The interviews, surveys, and journal entries created a layered picture of how motivation can affect inquiry and how teachers can maximize both in their classrooms. My final revelation, when all was said and done, was that I did, in fact, achieve my goal after all.

WORKS CITED

Duckworth, A. L., & Seligman, M. E. P. (2005). Self-discipline outdoes IQ in predicting academic performance of adolescents. *Psychological Science, 16*(12), 939–944.

Vallerand, R. J., Pelletier, L. G., Blais, M. R., Briere, N. M., Senecal, C., & Vallieres, E. F. (1992). The Academic Motivation Scale: A measure of intrinsic, extrinsic and amotivation in education. *Educational and Psychological Measurement, 52*, 1003–1017.

SECTION FIVE

Sharing THE Work

> Teacher research is a gift: to the profession, helping us change the way we see old problems and bringing us new solutions; to research communities, showing us new strategies and how to take risks in writing up research; to ourselves, reminding us of the energy and passion in learning that made us teachers in the first place.
>
> —SHAGOURY & POWER, 2012, P. 239

Too often, as teachers we struggle to find our voice. We are comfortable and confident using our voices in the classroom, but when it comes to policy discussions, reform initiatives, or advocacy, we find ourselves silenced. A prospective graduate student, describing her desire to pursue an advanced degree, recently related an incident where she had been in the room with a group of principals and superintendents. "I was really interested in what they were saying," she said, "but I didn't know how to participate. I didn't have the language to engage in the conversation."

Doing and sharing action research helps us find our voices. Systematically investigating our classroom practice, collecting and analyzing data, critically reading others' research, and talking through our work with students, colleagues, and mentors—all of these practices help to give us evidence and the language needed to engage in the conversation.

Our own studies following the experiences of graduates from our programs found that they demonstrated greater confidence when speaking with parents and administrators, a more analytical approach to district and state reforms, and a stronger voice as teacher leaders within their professional communities than did similarly positioned colleagues who had not participated in action research (Lattimer, 2012). One recent graduate, for example, explained,

> I think the experience really helped me to boost my confidence. For example, being confronted with issues like the principal saying, "Our AYP went down last year and we need to bring it up." Before, I think, I would have been totally intimidated, like, "Oh my gosh, how am I supposed to figure out strategies to improve test scores?" But having done AR, it's like, "OK, here's our research question, how do we analyze the data, how can we try new approaches and see what's working?" It helps you not to feel quite so overwhelmed by things like that.

At a time when mandates and test scores can paralyze and intimidate, AR is a powerful tool that can allow us to gain greater professional voice and take ownership of our practice. Of course, the potential for AR goes well beyond mandates, encouraging innovation and giving teachers the confidence to try new things and share their learning in a professional community. Another teacher, who is now a leader in her school and district in the area of project based learning (PBL), commented, "I don't think I would have ever tried incorporating project-based learning into my classroom if it hadn't been for AR. It provided me with the impetus, the structure, and the vision to try something new, carefully assess the impact, and then share my results with colleagues."

Sharing our research can also help keep us engaged in growing our own practice. "I was terrified the first time I presented at a professional conference," another recent graduate commented. She continued:

> When I sent in the proposal I never thought I'd get accepted, but I did, and then I actually had to get up in front of teachers from all over the country and share my AR. It was incredibly intimidating. But it turned out to be absolutely worth it. I learned so much from the experience. The questions that people asked really made me think, and I got connected to a network of teachers that I continue to learn from. Honestly, the whole experience of presenting and sharing my research has renewed and refocused me as a teacher. After a decade in the classroom, I was starting to feel burned out. Presenting my research linked me into a professional community that recharged my batteries and made me a much better educator.

The structures for how we share our work can range from the informal hallway conversation to more formal presentations at workshops or conferences. Writing up your work to share through professional journals, blogs, community newsletters, or websites can further strengthen your voice and expand your audience. Although it initially may seem intimidating, sharing your work publicly can be remarkably empowering. It provides a level of transparency that strengthens practice and connects you to a network of professional colleagues who value your voice. The four walls of a classroom can be remarkably isolating at times; sharing action research helps us to break out of that isolation and to provide a purpose for our work that extends beyond our individual classrooms.

Chapters in this final section of the book describe strategies for sharing findings and discuss the potential of action research as a tool for educational reform and sustainable professional and personal growth.

In the first chapter, Jennifer Edstrom confronts the challenge that nearly all of us experience when we sit down to write up our findings—the blinking cursor on an empty page. Writing is hard work, and, as practitioners, many of us are "doers" more than "tellers" and find the experience of writing up our findings to be especially challenging. Jennifer explores the obstacles that got in the way of her own writing and offers practical tips to help guide your work in progress. She positions her chapter as a call to action, encouraging teacher researchers to "raise your voice" to enact change for ourselves and our students.

Next, Alyssa Robledo-Graham describes the impact that her AR had on her school community. Student teaching in an urban school that she had graduated from only a few years earlier, Alyssa took on an AR challenge that confronted the norms of classroom discourse maintained by most teachers by challenging her students to engage in thoughtful, student-directed academic conversations. Her AR demonstrated to both Alyssa and her more experienced colleagues that students are capable of meeting high expectations, causing some to rethink their own practices and expectations for students.

Veronica Garcia's chapter, "Empowering Students as Change Agents: Reflections from a Social Justice Educator," also confronts misconceptions about urban students, from a slightly different approach—by engaging the students in conducting AR and then sharing their work with educators, community leaders, and policy makers. Veronica describes her work with a group of high school students who are part of UCLA's Council of Youth Research project. Her work mentoring these young researchers shifted community perceptions of urban students, students' perceptions of themselves, and Veronica's thinking about her own work as a classroom teacher.

Rob Meza-Ehlert's chapter, "Growing Our Practice: AR in a Professional Learning Community," explores the benefits and challenges of collaboratively engaging in action research with colleagues at his high school. The shared experience of coming together to research in their individual grade levels and content areas, review relevant literature, share classroom data, and collaboratively interrogate potential findings strengthened and sustained their work as both teachers and researchers, deepening their thinking and strengthening the professional discourse in their school.

Frank Cornelissen's chapter, "Getting Your Knowledge 'Out There': Finding Your Knowledge Ambassadors, or How They Find You" describes his work studying how teachers share their AR learning. His investigations of other action researchers found that their methods of sharing are often unconventional and unplanned, not confined to the standard research report or PowerPoint presentation at a conference. Frank gives his own account of finding a "knowledge ambassador" who would help him share his research, and then offers practical tips for other teacher researchers looking to get their work "out there."

Finally, Noriyuki Inoue's chapter, "Confessions of an Educational Researcher: Overcoming Cognitive Dissonance About Action Research," explores the concept of action research against the paradigm of research as a tool for uncovering universal truths. A trained empirical researcher, Nori was initially skeptical about the "squishiness" of action research, but shares that he has come to appreciate its value for uncovering the complexity of teaching and learning and for engaging teachers in shared professional growth.

As you read the accounts presented here, here are a few questions to consider as you think about your own teaching and research:

- How did these authors create change by sharing their research? Who was impacted? How did sharing research affect their own practice as teachers and researchers?
- What do you want to share about your own research? What are your goals in sharing your work?
- Who are the audiences for your research? How can you share your work in a way that is useful to them and that helps you achieve your broader goals?
- What platforms and strategies did the authors use for sharing their research? What are the pros and cons of each? Which might you use?
- What challenges did these authors encounter in seeking to share their research? How did they overcome those obstacles? What obstacles do you foresee in sharing your research, and how will you overcome them?
- What opportunities can you create to engage in professional conversations about your work?

Action research is rarely easy. It requires that we take risks, recognize challenges, be critical of our teaching, listen to our students, and be willing to adapt, adjust, and try again. It puts us into the role of expert in our own classroom, requiring us to design learning experiences for our students and then to honestly assess and take ownership of both their successes and our failures.

Sharing action research is not easy, either. It similarly requires that we take risks. It demands that we become more transparent about our practice and more willing to open ourselves to critique.

These are risks worth taking. Doing and sharing action research is engaging. It provides us with opportunities to look at our practice through new lenses, to hear different perspectives, and to grow in our own thinking. Doing and sharing action research is enriching. It allows us as classroom teachers who are often segmented and segregated from our colleagues to learn from one another to grow and improve our practice. And doing and sharing action research is empowering. It professionalizes our discourse and emboldens us to have a voice in conversations that are too often reserved for administrators or policy makers, conversations that directly impact our day-to-day practice and the lives of our students.

Certainly, AR is not a panacea. The authors of chapters throughout this book will tell you that their practice is still not perfect, and that they continue to face challenges each day. But AR is a tool that engages, enriches, and empowers us as educators to come together to strengthen our practice and our profession.

WORKS CITED

Lattimer, H. (2012). Action research in pre-service teacher education: Is there value added? *Inquiry in Education, 3*(1). Retrieved from http://digitalcommons.nl.edu/ie/vol3/iss1/5/

Shagoury, R., & Power, B. (2012). *Living the questions: A guide for teacher researchers* (2nd ed.). Portland, ME: Stenhouse.

CHAPTER TWENTY-FIVE

Raise Your Voice

Writing for Change, Writing to Be Heard

JENNIFER HARRIS EDSTROM

As I hit the stop button on my handheld voice recorder, one of the teachers with whom I had conducted my research turned to me and said, "You must feel relieved." I started at her blankly. She continued, "You are finished with your research." I nodded politely and smiled halfheartedly. I think my lack of enthusiasm was a little surprising and off-putting to her. *She was right. I should have been excited.* I had successfully facilitated two rounds of action research in the form of Japanese Lesson Study. The teachers with whom I worked had changed in their teaching practice as a result. The district administrators, who had supported this process from the beginning, were willing and interested in hearing about findings. *She was right. I should have been excited.* But, in truth, all I could feel was overwhelmed and, frankly, full of dread, because now the stop recording button had been hit. Now, the classroom portion was over. Now I had to write about the research.

Conducting the research was fun, but writing about it was a monumentally difficult task. As I sat at my desk, surrounded by journals, observation notes, 80 hours of voice recordings, and a looming deadline if I wanted to complete my degree on time, I could think of nothing I would rather do less than write about these findings. Instead, I cleaned out my home office. I straightened my desk. I filed paperwork. I organized my closet. I took my dog for endless walks. I returned to my now clean desk and stared at my computer screen, where a blank page taunted me. I was frozen with inaction. I felt overwhelmed by the sheer enormity of the data through which I would need to wade. Even more so, I was petrified that at the end of it all, my conclusions would be inconclusive or demonstrate to the academic world that I was just plain mediocre. I was the textbook definition of a "deer in the headlights." And then I had my realization. Writing up my research was more than simply meeting a requirement for my degree—it was an opportunity to raise my voice.

Action research, by design, is meant to be an empowering experience for educators. As a practitioner who had conducted my classroom research, I had now joined the ranks of experts who hold unique perspectives about learning, education, school environment, and unlimited other fundamental topics for educators, which can and must be shared with the world. I, as a professional, had the opportunity to share what I had learned, to draw conclusions, to change the field of education for the better. I had the chance, through my research, to be an educational reformer. It was the promise of being a change maker, a stakeholder, and an architect of the experience for students in my community that made this process so very appealing to me in the first place. However, I could be that kind of reformer only if I was willing to raise my voice. So I began to write. Through this process, I discovered many things about myself as a writer in general, and an academic writer specifically. As you raise your voice and share your work, consider the following lessons I learned during my own first foray into academic writing.

STAY CALM AND MAKE A LIST

Committing the voice of my research to paper was not easy. One of the most difficult parts of writing up the work was simply getting started. I was daunted by the bulk of the audio recordings I needed to transcribe, the observation journals I needed to reread, the conclusions I needed to encapsulate from the enormous amount of qualitative data. I sought out the advice of trusted friends and mentors who had written about their research in the past. The best advice I was given was "Just dive in." So I did. I listened to the recordings. I reread my journals. I paced my house. I asked myself over and over, "What did you notice? What made you think? Where were the challenges?"

My initial writing was simply to make a list of statements. As a new researcher, I did not have the confidence or experience to automatically see what my conclusions were, based off of my findings. I needed to find a method to make my way through the data and to make sense of it. The statements I wrote encapsulated what I thought I had found about a variety of aspects of education; I made bold statements about teaching, about learning, and about schools in general. Some of these were culled from the journal I had kept during the research process. Some of these were "Aha!" moments I had while listening to my tapes. I just put these ideas down on paper. I found that once I had a list of potential conclusions, I had something I could try to substantiate with the data I had collected. Many of these ideas became the key conclusions I highlighted in my paper, but some of these statements I could not support with my data. In those cases, I did not allow myself to become discouraged. Instead, I remained inspired to conduct the necessary research to explore those ideas in the future.

GET COMFORTABLE WITH THE MEDIUM

Although I knew the parts of an academic paper from research guides and handbooks, actually understanding what it meant to fill each of those sections was another story altogether. As I started to try to piece together my AR paper, I was reminded of a time during my undergraduate years when I took a studio art survey course. During the course of the semester, we explored six different paint mediums. Having painted with acrylic paint in art class for years, I felt pretty confident about my artistic ability. However as I was introduced to oil paints, watercolors, and encaustic, I felt like I was holding a paintbrush for the first time. I had to learn to be comfortable with each new medium, coming to understand what each paint felt like when placed on canvas or paper. I needed to practice, experiment, and become immersed in each before I felt my creativity and artistic voice sing out again.

In truth, the same could be said about academic writing. By the time I conducted my research, I felt like a seasoned writer. I had breezed through graduate papers and had a long track record of successful writing experiences. I did not really feel like the writing itself would be problematic. However, academic writing in which I was capturing new ideas and my own original conclusions left me feeling like one of my former 4th-grade students encountering the 5-paragraph essay for the first time. I was out of my element.

Stepping back, I realized that models were all around me. Writing, even with a distinct author's voice and style layered into it, is formulaic. The components of this formula were at my fingertips; I had read hundreds of examples when conducting my lit review. I had spent 2 years reading academic papers prior to conducting my research in graduate school. Now it was my turn to join these ranks of academic writers, but I needed to revisit their work as inspiration and guidance and reread them as a fellow author, looking at how the writing was structured, how ideas were developed, and how voice was captured. I found myself going back to those that were similar to my research in design and rereading them. I concentrated on the findings and conclusions sections alone. How had other researchers I admired captured their findings and written about them in a compelling way? I spent several days rereading findings and conclusions. After immersing myself in these sections I had a sense of how I wanted to write my own. The formula had clicked into place. I still had the space in which to capture my own voice, my own conclusions, and my own ideas. But I had other successful examples of writing to guide me when putting my words on paper.

BE TRUE TO YOURSELF

While using the examples of others to guide me in my writing was an essential kick-start to my first academic writing, I must admit that there were some unforeseen consequences to becoming immersed in the work of others. The first clue that I was in trouble was when I wrote the following sentence, "The oeuvre of academic exploration focused on professionalism is vast, however an authentic understanding of what it is to be a professional educator is still in need of elucidation." It is true. I used the words *oeuvre, vast,* and *elucidation* in one sentence. I pride myself on possessing a great vocabulary, but what was I trying to accomplish? Fortunately, a trustworthy reader pointed out to me that this sentence seemed "a bit much." I rewrote it, and in the process, had another moment of insight. I discovered that I very easily become a mimic, and I also have the tendency to fall into some unfortunate grandiloquence when I am trying to write the way I had imagined an academic should. I am still shaking my head over *oeuvre.*

It is certainly true that academic writing is different than other types of writing. There is a need for the purposeful use of effective vocabulary to provide a carefully crafted argument. However, equally important is that those words have a ring of authenticity. Without that foundation, an author runs a risk that the conclusions he or she has made will be perceived as less than convincing. If I am taking the time to research, put my findings together, and put together conclusions that may change the face of education, then I want to be credible. I want my writing to serve as the bridge between my ideas and the reader, rather than act as an obstacle.

Furthermore, an author may risk his or her work in far more critical ways if the writing is too obscure. Early in graduate school I found myself reading a key paper by a famous and respected educational theorist. I spent hours reading and rereading this paper, trying to make heads or tails of what this noted educational thought leader was trying to say. I was determined to understand it, and I eventually came to have a passable comfort with its contents. However, my prevailing thought at the end of reading this was, "How on earth did this person ever get enough readers to become mainstream?" I am willing to let go of my reader believing that I am erudite or some kind of educational genius, because at the end of the day I want to *have readers.* I have to consider who those readers might be. As a practitioner raising my voice to share my research, I am most interested in sharing this work with other teachers, policy makers, and education leaders. The reality is that they may not possess either the time or inclination to read through cumbersome academic writing. Finding an academic voice that rings true and clear is not easy. Consider rereading writing aimed at practitioners rather than theorists to get a sense of how others have created that user-friendly and authentic voice. Trusted readers that know you, your style, and your convictions are a valuable resource to have, as they can keep you true to yourself and help you avoid the temptation of gross verbosity or inauthentic style.

LET GO OF YOUR PREDICTIONS

When I was an elementary school student, I used to love to participate in science fairs. I enjoyed choosing a topic to explore, creating a hypothesis, and testing it. I especially loved when my hypothesis lined up with my findings. I will never forget the elation I experienced when, as predicted, one particular mouthwash was most effective at killing bacteria of the mouth. It was so black-and-white, so cut-and-dried, so nicely tied-up-with-a-bow! Now, writing up my action research conclusions, I craved that kind of resolution. I had some very clear predictions about what I thought my research would tell me about teachers and their professionalism. I wanted a clear-cut answer to determine the validity of my hypothesis. I felt like I had matured since those early science experiments in school, for in truth, I did not even really care if my hypothesis was proven to be true or not true. I just wanted an answer, either way. Still, when I made that early list of big ideas, I found myself sticking to my preconceived notions of what I had assumed I would find. However, when I went to support these conclusions with my actual data, I found that my supporting evidence was actually fairly thin. I had a panicked conversation with a faculty advisor who calmed me with the sagacity that comes with research experience. Over the course of our conversation, I realized that I had a lot that I could conclude that was deeply supported by my data—it just was not what I anticipated I would conclude.

Sticking within the confines of my predictions would have truly sold my research short. The beauty of action research is that it is organic, flexible, and has a soul of its own. As my data and findings unfolded, I found that there were incredibly important conclusions that could be drawn about professionalism and teachers that I could never have conceived of when designing my project. I had far more information about school culture and environment than ever before, and as I worked through my data, it was the lessons I learned about this impact that was most significant. Learning to let go and be open to the possibilities of what research can yield was one of the most exciting and enriching parts of conducting action research.

BE A DIPLOMAT, BUT AN HONEST ONE

If one of the key reasons we write about our work is to raise our voices for educational improvement, then we have to share our conclusions with the educators around us and beyond. That is great in theory, but as is the case with many things, in practice it is not so easy. As I wrapped up my conclusions about my action research study, I was so excited and blown away by my findings and conclusions about a school culture and environment's impact on teacher professionalism that I wanted to shout them from the rooftops. I had discovered there were structural limitations to teachers' increasing their professionalism. I had data to support it. I was onto something. We could make change based on this! Except there was one problem—the picture I was painting of the school environment in which I had conducted the research was not always so rosy and flattering. My writing would have to reflect many district- and school-implemented policies and their sometimes negative effects on teachers. And then, as I had promised when I began the research, I would be expected to stand up in front of district and school administrators and share these sometimes hard-to-hear findings. I was terrified. I felt like a tightrope walker scaling a piece of fraying thread over a pit of alligators.

It is a balancing act to tell the truth, and to do so in a way that does not alienate or shut down conversations around the very tables where change can be made. I knew that for teachers in this district to grow as professionals, some changes to existing policies would need to take place. However, I also knew that if I came in throwing accusations and data at the district, I was likely to meet with defensiveness and deaf ears. I decided to tell the truth, but to do so with care. Once again, I enlisted trusted advisors to read my work and presentations for potential land mines in my writing. I practiced my presentations with my audience in mind. I was honest, but I was careful not to point fingers. We have an obligation as action researchers to report our findings and to help make change for our students, but we need to do so in a sensible and sensitive way.

I raised my voice about teacher professionalism in one school and in one district. I overcame my writer's block. I became more comfortable with my voice as an academic writer. I learned to hone my writing to tell an honest and effective story that argues for change—and some change did happen as a result of my work. The district continues to support the facilitation of action research in its schools. District policies are under examination and efforts are being made to better empower teachers. It is change by a fraction of an inch, but that fraction of an inch might not have occurred if I had not raised my voice by writing and sharing my work. I am inspired by the idea of how many miles those little fractions of inches could add up to if we as educators together were to collectively raise our voices about our teaching and research. Talk about empowerment!

CHAPTER TWENTY-SIX

Challenging Assumptions

A Student Teacher's Action Research Prompts Veterans to Rethink Their Beliefs about K–12 Student Potential

ALYSSA ROBLEDO-GRAHAM

A PASSION TO CREATE CHANGE

My decision to focus my action research on student-centered discussion strategies in urban settings was prompted by my own secondary educational experience. I am a product of the same district in which I now work; I actually conducted my action research at the same high school from which I graduated 6 years earlier. Looking back to my high school experiences in the classroom, "learning" was achieved through repetition and was heavily dependent upon textbooks.

In the majority of my high school classes the teacher stood at the front of the class and lectured while we sat in individual desks that were organized in straight rows. In most cases we worked individually, completing worksheets and highly structured essays. In English, it was vocabulary, grammar exercises, and papers on the literature read in class. It was only after entering college, in my first English course, that I was introduced to a class discussion on literature. It was then that I realized that I had been cheated in high school, where the "discussions" that took place in my classroom were like video clips taken from a Charlie Brown cartoon. Either a dialogue occurred between the teacher and a couple of "good" students, or the teacher was met with the deafening sound of silence and answered her own questions.

Now, as I transition into the role of teacher myself, early observations make it apparent that little has changed in the intervening years since I graduated high school. In 9th grade you still read Shakespeare's *Romeo and Juliet* and are expected to memorize lines from the play. In 10th grade you read Elie Wiesel's *Night*, write a paper, and watch many movies. The patterns continued, and based on student feedback, it is clear that many perceive the readings and writing assignments in English as meaningless and predictable.

For many of my former teachers, who are now my soon-to-be colleagues, the mentality is, "If it ain't broke, don't fix it." However, what many have failed to see is that it *is* broken; students are bored, courses have fallen into a rut, and learning is less than it should be, particularly since many of these students could represent the first generation in their families to attend college. Things need to change, and educators need to be implementing new teaching and learning strategies, so that our urban students feel prepared and not cheated.

NAVIGATING CHANGE AS A NOVICE TEACHER RESEARCHER

As a novice teacher and a first-time teacher researcher I was well aware of the potentially precarious position I was placing myself in by electing to take on an action research project that ran contrary to the norms of the school. I recognize the fact that I have a lot to learn from my colleagues. Those that I called my teachers are now my mentors, and I am grateful that they have opened up their classrooms and willingly shared with me the wisdom that comes from their years of experience. However, part of my rationale for coming back to teach in the school where I was once a student was to work to create change that would improve outcomes for students, and I wanted to do more than simply maintain the status quo.

As I began to develop my AR I had a conversation with a colleague about my research focus. I explained that I was making changes and veering from a teacher-led class toward a classroom driven by the students. I enthusiastically went into detail about the strategies I was planning to implement that I hoped would result in a more student-centered learning environment. Her response was one of bewilderment. She asked "Why?" and my response was "Why not?" My colleague explained that it would be too difficult to try something like that with the type of kids we have at this school. It is hard enough trying to have them learn the curriculum, she explained. She then shook her head and wished me good luck.

Excited and nervous, I began the transition process from a traditional, teacher-centered classroom to a student-centered learning environment. I found solace in the fact that even if my student-centered discussion strategies failed, that did not make me or my students failures. A professor of mine shared that early on in her teaching career, her mentor explained that it was better to try new things and fail than never to try anything at all. I took this to heart and decided that my philosophy on teaching would be about risk, faith, patience, and practice.

WITNESSING CHANGE IN MY OWN CLASSROOM

Little by little, the changes that I was implementing in my classroom began to have an impact on students. As we integrated Socratic seminars, fishbowl discussions, and reciprocal teaching into the day-to-day class norms, students began to engage more thoughtfully with the subject, to develop their speaking, listening, and analysis skills, and to change their perceptions of themselves. No longer were they just "urban" kids; now they were readers and thinkers who could participate in thoughtful conversations. They were developing confidence and voice.

In my master's program one of the texts that most resonated for me was Paulo Freire's *Pedagogy of the Oppressed* (1970). In it he described the typical teacher-centered classroom as a "banking" process in which

> knowledge is a gift bestowed by those who consider themselves knowledgeable upon those whom they consider know nothing. Projecting an absolute ignorance upon others, a characteristic of the ideology of oppression, negates education and knowledge as a processes of inquiry. The teacher presents himself to his students as their necessary opposite; by considering their ignorance as absolute, he justifies his own existence. (p. 5)

I knew that in my own classroom I wanted to upend the banking process of teaching, recognize the knowledge that students bring with them to school, and co-construct deeper understandings together. But as a new teacher, I had reservations, because many of my more experienced colleagues feared change and doubted it was possible. Was I being naïve? Was it really possible to create change in this classroom with these students?

What I witnessed through my AR taught me that student-centered discussion strategies like Socratic seminars, fishbowl discussions, and reciprocal teaching matter because they change banking pedagogy. My research demonstrated that when I used these techniques they had a positive impact on my classroom. The students became active and engaged in real discussions, with and without the teacher. They were active in constructing knowledge, and most importantly, they improved student attitude and self-image. After my class made the transition to student-centered discussion strategies, I saw an increase in meaningful discussion, improved self-image, and a challenge for my students. The students were in control of what they wanted to discuss and worked together to develop meaning for a text.

Although I might have made some of these changes on my own, AR provided a structure and a vehicle to document and witness the power of student-centered learning. It helped me clarify my thinking, identify concerns, and systematically collect evidence that compellingly demonstrated the power and potential of my urban students.

ADVOCATING FOR CHANGE IN MY SCHOOL

As I watched my students and my classroom transform, I wanted to share it with my colleagues. However, after the less-than-enthusiastic reception that my early ideas about student-centered discussion strategies had received, I was initially reluctant to talk too much about the changes that were happening in my classroom. Although I was incredibly proud of my students and our work together, I didn't want to come across as a know-it-all newbie. But word of our work leaked out.

From early on, I had been transparent with the students about what we were doing and why. As they began to see the success, they felt empowered to share our achievements with other students and teachers. Soon, teachers began to ask questions, and a few asked to visit the classroom. Always aware of my junior teacher status, I was careful to ask for their feedback and insights from their observations. I didn't want to be seen as "showing off"; instead, I viewed the opportunity to share and get feedback from more experienced colleagues as a way of engaging in a community of practice that would strengthen all of our understandings.

What my colleagues witnessed when observing students in my classroom confronted many of their expectations and assumptions about what urban students can do. Although few would openly acknowledge it, many of the teachers at my school bought into an approach that Martin Haberman (1991) describes as the "pedagogy of poverty," an assumption that "teaching is what teachers do and learning is what students do … a pedagogy in which learners can 'succeed' without becoming either involved or thoughtful" (p. 4). Although this approach had "worked" for the school for many years, allowing them to demonstrate proficiency in memorization-reliant standardized test scores, it failed to adequately prepare our students with the knowledge, skills, dispositions, and social capital needed to succeed in college and careers. Many teachers believed that they were protecting students by not demanding that they engage more actively in their learning; they didn't believe that students were capable. Sharing my action research disrupted many of these beliefs.

Doing action research at my high school and having the opportunity to share it resulted in my colleagues' changing their minds. Today, I see that they are trying new things because of the research that I did and the results they witnessed. A lot of teachers doubted. I was told, "not with these students," "not in this area." What my AR proved was that I could create change and challenge students to do more. And if I, the novice, could do it, then maybe they could do it too. Taking on a controversial topic in a school that too often was comfortable with complacency was a risk, especially for a novice teacher. But it was a risk that paid off, and it has led to positive change and higher expectations for my students, my colleagues, and the larger school community.

WORKS CITED

Freire, P. (1970). *Pedagogy of the oppressed.* New York: Continuum.

Haberman, M. (1991). The pedagogy of poverty versus good teaching. *Phi Delta Kappan, 73*(4), 290–294.

CHAPTER TWENTY-SEVEN

Empowering Students As Change Agents

Reflections from a Social Justice Educator

VERONICA GARCIA

It's a warm afternoon during the summer of 2008, and I am with my team of four high school student researchers from the UCLA Council of Youth Research. We have spent the day in the local neighborhood of El Sereno in Northeast Los Angeles interviewing and videotaping impromptu conversations with members of the community—students and adults. We have visited community organizations and walked the local streets, seeking answers to our research questions from those who are directly impacted by education and other critical social issues. The title of our research project is "One Step Forward, Two Steps Back: Stressful Times at Wilson High School." The students are investigating how the economic crisis in California has impacted students, teachers, and families. They have taken the lead throughout the day, and I am there to provide support as they engage with the community on a much deeper level. I continue to be humbled by their confidence and expertise, as I observe them tackling serious social issues that directly impact their lives.

As the day heats up we take a break at the home of Erick, one of the student researchers. His family has made homemade tacos, rice, and beans, a truly delicious meal. We have also arranged to interview Erick's parents, both immigrants to the U.S. from Mexico, for our action research project. My students and I gather around in their living room and Erick's parents sit on the couch. We divide up the roles on our team, so the students situate themselves according to what they will do during the interview. Two of the students are the interviewers and sit across the couch from Erick's parents. Erick is the videographer and has set up the camera across from his parents. Two others are note takers and will capture additional notes during the interview. The interview begins and Erick's parents speak warmly to us in Spanish as they answer my students' questions.

My student researchers and I listen intently to their stories, as they tell us about their hopes and dreams for their only son. They came to the U.S. as immigrants and have worked hard to provide for Erick as best they can. They have minimal years of formal education because they have worked most of their lives. They are most proud of Erick because he does so well in school and will be the first to attend college. My students nod their heads in agreement as Erick's parents speak, because they too are first-generation students whose parents came to this country for opportunity and a better life for their families. Before we leave, the students thank Erick's parents for welcoming us into their home and providing us with a home-cooked meal. It is in these moments of direct, human contact with the community and youth that learning and reflection takes place for both students and teachers like me. It is in these moments that the transformative power of action research is realized and changes the way educators like me think about the role we have and the work we do both inside and outside the classroom.

That summer afternoon is ingrained in my memory. For several years, I had the opportunity to serve as a lead teacher in the UCLA Council of Youth Research (CYR). During the time, I was also a high school English teacher with Los Angeles Unified School District. In the CYR, students conduct participatory action research in teams during the school year and summer, on problems they identify in their schools and communities throughout Los Angeles. The final product is a documentary that is presented to the superintendent, administrators, principals, community organizations, parents, and students.

Our action research projects over the years have addressed issues of school climate, student-teacher relationships, peer relationships, school resources/funding, curriculum, and local community needs. The projects have given our students a voice and platform to be leaders, and have led to real change in their schools and communities. And they have also led to tremendous learning for those of us who led the work, supporting our development as classroom teachers and social justice educators.

IMPACT OF AR ON THE COMMUNITY

There is an abundance of negative stereotypes of urban working-class youth of color in the media, news, and, unfortunately, in our classrooms and schools. Engaging in action research with my students was critical in changing how adults perceived these young people. As students engaged with city leaders, politicians, and administrators for interviews, for example, these officials could not help but voice their surprise at what the students were doing. When students presented their final reports and PowerPoints at Los Angeles City Hall, or in the superintendent's office in Boston, or at the prestigious American Educational Research Association (AERA) conference, consistently the responses noted how powerful it was to see youth taking on such critical issues and being so thorough in their investigations. Other classroom teachers often commented about my students and how well they did, which contradicted their negative perceptions of the students in their classrooms. They often could not believe these students were doing "this kind of quality work." When students presented their work to my teacher colleagues, it helped to change perceptions of the students as leaders, critical thinkers, and intellectuals, and this ultimately helped teachers consider new ways of working with students. Having students who are most often marginalized and stereotyped demonstrate what they *can* do upended the deficit perspective with which urban students are often viewed, and showed the potential of our youth to be successful when they are provided with opportunities and support.

IMPACT OF AR ON THE STUDENTS

In addition to changing how adults perceived our students, action research also changed how students perceived *themselves*. Many of the students who participated in my AR groups over the years did not have history of academic success or civic engagement. Rather, most were struggling academically, and experienced other challenging circumstances at home and in their communities. Some of them had never been to a college campus, and now in CYR, they were spending their summer in a UCLA lecture hall.

Action research supports students' transformations because students are in charge of the investigations, and that search for answers is rooted in their lived experiences. Too often, high school students are provided the information in their classrooms from textbooks and seemingly irrelevant course material. In AR, students bring the knowledge and information, which validates their sense of being. They feel confident in being able to contribute to discussions, respond to literature, and draw conclusions about evidence. The intensity and level of engagement in one's life and community has a powerful role in helping students recognize that they carry a wealth of knowledge and skills that were never recognized before. They come to realize that they are *smart*, and capable of reading and writing about academic literature (that most of us do not read until graduate school), interviewing adults in high-level positions with confidence, and presenting to packed audiences their solutions to issues that directly impact them and their families. I saw firsthand how many of my students changed the way they engaged in their classrooms. In being more informed of the academic and social issues, they became empowered to challenge their school experiences.

IMPACT OF AR ON MY DEVELOPMENT AS AN EDUCATOR

Being a part of the action research took me directly into the community to interact with families and other youth and community members. In the Council of Youth Research we were assigned to the communities in which we taught to more effectively support our schools' students, most of whom were also on our research teams. I was always assigned to El Sereno, the location of the high school where I was a teacher. Being able to stay close to my school's community during the summer gave me a unique opportunity to know my students and their families. I probably would not have gone into their neighborhoods or into their homes on my own, since the norm is that families come to the school, not the other way around. Thanks to the AR work with students, each summer, I was pushed to reach out in more authentic ways to the community. I developed relationships with local community members, business owners, and parents because of the close interactions we had during the summer. I found that parents also felt appreciated, and valued that their son or daughter's teacher would come to their home or neighborhood and not be so disconnected. Even if my Spanish was not great, I would make the effort to communicate as best I could, which was also appreciated by the parents, because I at least tried. Some of the relationships I established during the summer carried over into the school year, and I invited these individuals to my classroom as guests. The discomfort I felt about developing relationships with families and the broader community, which I had been unable to process or take the initiative to confront, was ultimately eased through AR and the students. I had better relationships with families, and I could also be an advocate for them and work against negative perceptions or stereotypes that existed among some staff at my school.

AR also supported my pedagogical development. I became a more thoughtful and organized teacher when creating units and lessons around problem solving and critical thinking. I provided opportunities for students to share their realities with one another to support their achievement and get them engaged. I was more open and willing to make my classroom one that modeled the types of experiences my students and I had during the summers. I was explicit in calling my students experts, and made sure that lessons asked them to think about how the literature or issues or questions we discussed related back to their lives. I searched for more relevant material to complement my units. Most importantly, I always made an effort to invite adults to participate in my classroom. For example, during individual persuasive speeches or group presentations, I invited the principal, literacy coaches, community members, or even other colleagues to hear what my students were learning. We also presented several times to education classes at UCLA, in front an audience of graduate students. These experiences were similar to the efforts we made in CYR (when students in the council presented at Los Angeles City Hall to a packed room)—the powerful outcomes of those efforts encouraged me to bring it to my own classroom. Giving students the opportunity to speak in front of adults ultimately changed people's stereotypical views of them, and showed the potential they have if they are provided with the appropriate foundation. I have so many positive memories of classroom discussions and students working together in my classroom, because of how AR impacted my thinking about pedagogy, curriculum, relationships, and achievement.

In *Pedagogy of the Oppressed* Paulo Freire wrote, "In problem-posing education, people develop their power to perceive critically the way they exist in the world with which and in which they find themselves; they come to see the world not as a static reality, but as a reality in process, in transformation" (1970, p. 83). At the heart of this quote is the concept of transformation. Engaging in action research alongside my students with the Council of Youth Research transformed who I am as a person and the kind of educator I want to be. It made me a more passionate advocate for youth voice and critical reflection. It transformed my classroom by acknowledging students as the experts and the importance of establishing relationships with families. It transformed my students, their perceptions of themselves, and their aspirations. And it confronted long-standing stereotypes about urban youth, causing educators, administrators, and policy makers to rethink their preconceptions.

WORKS CITED

Freire, P. (1970). *Pedagogy of the oppressed.* New York: Continuum.

CHAPTER TWENTY-EIGHT

Growing Our Practice

AR in a Professional Learning Community

ROBERT MEZA-EHLERT

Change has always been scary for me. I often find it easier to talk about new ideas and approaches than actually to embrace them. Talking is safe, but doing? Now, that's another thing altogether. Even though I've helped to launch a project-based school known for its innovative approaches, I often balk when faced with challenges and transitions that require making a leap into new territory. Many times I use questions to rationalize and form a hedge of protection between my practice and the unknown: *Isn't my current approach good enough? Aren't my students' scores already improving? Where will I find time to do that? Don't I work hard enough already?* In a recent school year, I "found my courage" to embrace change by inviting other teachers to join me in viewing our classrooms through an action research lens. Deciding *together* that we would *all* take risks in order to improve student outcomes opened up a path to real transformation in my own mindset. The results were often mixed, but for me, the power of engaging in shared action research was found in the rich experience of dialogue, accountability, and inquiry in collaboration with my colleagues.

Although I've used action research on my own and even taught action research methods courses to new teachers in a university setting, this was the first time that I engaged in collaborative AR with my colleagues. The experience taught me that I'm at my best when I am trying new things in the classroom, and that a team is the best catalyst to get me moving in a fresh direction.

SHIFTING THE STATUS QUO

Imagine a typical classroom in the early morning hours before students arrive on campus. The smell of coffee and warm cinnamon rolls is in the air. Teachers sit in a circle, discussing an article about the importance of academic language in student writing. As they share their insights and classroom experiences, the laughter reveals a sense of community and camaraderie.

This scene describes a typical meeting of my school's monthly "Reading & Discussion" group. The group members included teachers from a range of grades and disciplines who had voluntarily come together out of a shared interest in talking about our practice in a collaborative setting. This was a "bottom up" gathering—no administrative mandates, open to all who were interested in informal and thoughtful conversation. Our discussions often inspired us to try something new in our classrooms, but as a group, we had never established a clear focus on application and accountability, so more often than not, we'd be back around the table the following month enjoying our coffee cake and discussion without any measurable risk, growth, or transformation for us or for our students. We had actually reached a danger zone, as an officially recognized National Blue Ribbon School. Our "good enough" had been officially deemed good enough, so where was the need for change?

Aware of this potential for stagnation, during our September meeting a few years ago, I suggested that we shift our group's purpose to focus on action research. After a few minutes of establishing together what that would mean, the group agreed to try out a new direction. We kept the "R & D" name, but adopted "Research & Development" as the new title for the group. Reading and discussion would certainly take place, but in a targeted way, with improved student outcomes as the goal. It was frightening for me to take that first step and offer the suggestion that we pursue an active research mindset, because I knew that I was stepping into a more vulnerable place that could move in any number of directions. However, once the group was behind the idea, the next steps felt far easier because there was a sense that we were in this together.

WHICH WAY TO THE CHANGE?

I felt unsure, at first, how to lead the process of collaborative action research, but soon turned to the concept of backward planning, which proved to be an invaluable starting place. Beginning with the end in mind, we asked the question, "What characteristics should all students at our school exhibit by the time they are graduating seniors?" We were soon able to streamline our list down to a half dozen characteristics. Of these, two stood out as particularly relevant across all subject areas:

- Work ethic: managing time and effort for success
- Dissatisfaction with mediocrity: pushing for excellence

The next step of our process involved reviewing professional and research literature to gather wisdom from others in the field who had looked at ways to increase student success in these same areas.

Our December and January R & D discussions had a deep impact on me. We were reading articles not merely to discuss them, but to apply the insights of others to our own unique situations. We read more closely and reflected more deeply because the work *really* mattered. These sessions shaped and refined the interventions that each teacher designed in response to their unique classroom settings. One teacher eventually decided to have his AP European history students write up a daily work plan at the start of each class, complete with an outline of steps to refocus or extend their learning at key points in the class session. Another created a daily evaluation form for her sophomore digital media classes so that students could slow down and reflect on their achievements for the day, as well as set new goals for the next class meeting. Other teachers approached the issue less from a personal management angle and more from a metacognitive one. One colleague had her students reflect on which habits of mind they used in the process of completing and revising essays for her American literature classes. Another teacher created space in her AVID class for students to reflect not only on key content they had learned in their core classes that week, but also on how revision was central to the process of producing high-level work.

FROM CLASSROOM MANAGEMENT TO STUDENT SELF-MANAGEMENT

In my own world history classes, I observed that many students needed a system to help them slow down and take control of their management of assignments. A number of my students turned homework in only sporadically, and often failed to submit in-class assignments they had actually completed. At the end of a unit, as we prepared for a Socratic seminar and summative writing piece, students often seemed unaware of the rich resources available through the assignments they had already completed. One day, after a solid week of studying the Enlightenment thinkers, Veronica asked the dreaded question, "Where should I get the information for this stuff? Should I just Google it?" Veronica's question (and numerous others like it) sparked my own list of questions: How does a student at the end of a unit forget entirely about the resources we've worked so hard on? Why do so many students not turn in homework? Are they aware of how our grading categories work? Would students respond better to different assignments? How can I increase students' organizational skills? I felt a sense of desperation for many of my students, because it wasn't as if they got the big ideas and simply forgot to turn in a homework assignment. Instead, many students were struggling to make meaning of the content, and it felt to me that there was a huge disconnect between what I saw as my carefully planned and purposeful activities and their (apparent) perception that the work didn't hold much meaning or usefulness.

My approach to dealing with this disconnect was shaped by Peg Dawson's (2010) challenge to distinguish so-called "laziness" from a lack of "executive skills" in our students. I began having students complete a daily work journal in which students simply logged the date, assignment, and notes of the assignment's purpose. I hoped that by ending each class session with time to keep track of assignments, students would be more likely to submit their work, more cognizant of the flow of our learning, and able to access previous assignments to help with writing or seminar preparation at the end of a unit.

A few weeks into my process of looking at how daily work logs impacted student learning, the R & D group met again to discuss ReLeah Cossett Lent's (2010) focus on teachers handing over more responsibility for student success to the students themselves, and Kathleen Cushman's (2010) examination of the necessary elements to inspire teens to push themselves towards perfection. In the midst of the discussion, a colleague challenged me to keep the process student-centered by simply asking them how their daily work logs were working. Paired with the readings, my colleague's gentle suggestion led me to a signature learning moment of my AR experience that year—what others might label as an "Ah-ha!" moment, but which I call my "Oh, duh!" moment, for the sheer obviousness of it in retrospect. I had designed a "fix" for my students without ever seriously consulting their opinions on what would work best for them. This "Oh, duh!" moment would likely never have arrived had I not been engaged in this work collaboratively with colleagues. And the realization had a major impact on my classroom practice.

The next day, I had students complete a quick write on the topic, and it was immediately clear that they either wanted to do away with the daily logs altogether or make our use of them much more specific and detailed. I chose to stick with the daily logs, and with the help of a small team of student leaders created a new log with space for students to track the submission status of the assignment, their grade, and notes on the big idea of the assignment to help them understand its usefulness. As part of the new arrangement, I had to adapt my grading and feedback patterns to accommodate my students' desire for a faster turnaround. This was part of that uncomfortable new territory I had feared, but I was convinced that meaningful, timely feedback would help increase student learning. We eventually developed a pattern for the remainder of the semester that consisted of consulting the daily log at the start and close of each class period; we would begin each session by tracking assignment submissions and feedback, and at the end we would ensure that students were aware of their new responsibilities and due dates.

RESULTS: NUMBERS AND BEYOND

The use of the daily log seems to have made a positive impact on student success in my classes, but like any intervention, the results were as varied as my diverse group of students. In one of my world history classes, work completion went up 43% over the previous grading period, and eventually, seven students who failed the first semester passed in the second. There was Ramon, who "came to life" and began taking responsibility for his success in my class. Ramon's assignment completion went from 11% in the first semester to 72% in the second semester, with a corresponding jump in test scores from 38% to 67%. The influence spread beyond my class, as two colleagues requested that I share my revised daily journal sheet with them because they had overheard students talking about how it helped them keep track of their effort and performance. An honest look at the intervention, however, revealed a much more muddled picture: Too many students still failed my class, more than half of students whose work completion increased saw little or no jump in exam or writing scores, and as the semester waned, so did many students' assignment submission rates.

When I shared my results with my colleagues in the R & D group throughout the spring, I found similar patterns emerging from their classroom inquiries. There were a number of individual breakthrough moments for students, and positive trends in learning, but these were always tempered by the reality that there was no one solution that worked for every teacher or every student. The powerful shift, however, was that together we were researching, designing, implementing, and adapting targeted interventions that directly impacted students. We gained a sense of empowerment because rather than simply commiserating about an issue, we were actively identifying and trying ways to increase student success.

The shared AR process renewed my belief that my responsiveness to student need is a critical factor in determining whether my learners will find success or be overwhelmed in a downward spiral of failure. Walking through this process with my colleagues shaped a core value in my approach to teaching by getting me to value asking the students for their input as we build a learning community together. One certainty as I move forward in my career is that there will always be students who struggle with content, skills, and organization. I want to be that teacher who listens and responds to my students' needs. I want to be that teacher who adapts my systems and pedagogy to maximize their opportunity to learn. Collaborative action research has been a key component of helping me push through my fear of change and become more the teacher that my students need me to be.

WORKS CITED

Cushman, K. (2010). The strive of it. *Educational Leadership, 67*(5), 50–55.

Dawson, P. (2010). Lazy—or not? *Educational Leadership, 68*(2), 35–38.

Lent, R. C. (2010). The responsibility breakthrough. *Educational Leadership, 68*(1), 68–71.

CHAPTER TWENTY-NINE

Getting Your Knowledge "Out There"

Finding Your Knowledge Ambassadors, or How They Find You

FRANK CORNELISSEN

How do you get the knowledge from your action research "out there"? How can colleagues and other educators benefit from what you've found in your study? These were questions I asked educators involved in action research. My study was a so-called "second-person" action research study: researching the first-person experiences of other action researchers.

Doing research on research—it seems a little bit like Russian dolls. Every time you open one, another one is inside. This is what happened in my study, too. Every time the action researchers shared with me their drive for sharing their knowledge, their successes, and bumpy moments, it resonated with my own experiences, thoughts, and feelings as a researcher. I shared their passion for strengthening educational practice and their feelings of great joy and satisfaction when others valued their research findings. I also shared their struggles with getting their research knowledge out to those who could use it.

As I talked to fellow action researchers, I noticed that the most powerful strategies they cited for sharing their work were often informal, unstructured, and unplanned. These ways of sharing did not take place in the traditional ways, by handing someone a structured research report, or during invited presentations for team meetings or conferences, but in informal social settings, through spontaneous collaboration, unexpected connections, enthusiastic conversations, and small talk in the hallway. Often, there was a special person—an advisor, colleague, or friend—who helped share the researcher's work. This person seemed like a kind of ambassador for the knowledge and ideas that they had developed in their research. This knowledge ambassador was convinced of the value of their knowledge and enthusiastically talked to their colleagues, school director, and other educators and directed them to the action researcher and his/her findings. These knowledge ambassadors were important connectors who helped the action researchers to disseminate their work.

After hearing these stories, I became convinced that I needed such a knowledge ambassador for my study too! But, who could it be? I knew it should be someone I have a good relationship with, who is familiar with my study, convinced of its value, a good connector, and of course, willing to support me in sharing my work. Where to find someone like this? I hadn't found such a person among my colleagues. People were often polite about my study and its findings. They called it interesting and valuable, but I felt no real engagement with further sharing or using the work. Where else could I look? I had no clue.

My knowledge ambassador revealed herself during a conference. My spouse, Marieke, and I were attending a conference on action research in beautiful and sunny San Diego. Being Dutch, we appreciated this change of weather. At the conference, I gave some presentations about my study. I enjoyed them, but the real sharing of my study happened somewhere else, and I wasn't even present.

Marieke was still waking up, on the terrace enjoying the morning sun and drinking some coffee after our late arrival the day before, when a woman joined her at the table and started talking. They had a pleasant conversation and Marieke enthusiastically talked about the study that I was presenting. They noticed there was a connection between my study topic and the school setting where the woman was working. The woman even invited us to come to her school to see things with our own eyes and talk further.

That night, Marieke told me about the nice woman she had met, how interesting and unique her school setting was, how well it seemed to connect to my study and findings, and the invitation the woman had extended to visit. Maybe we could go the day after the conference? Now, you would think that I would enthusiastically say, "Yes, of course! Let's go and see!" I wish I could say that I said that, but to be honest (and somewhat ashamed) I said that I'd rather go to the famous San Diego Zoo. Over the next hour, Marieke convinced me to go, and in the end we decided to go to the school in the morning (and not stay too long) and to the zoo in the afternoon.

The visit to the school was a turning point in my research. To make a long story short: We didn't make it to the zoo, but we made a valuable connection with people doing similar work, and the school became one of the settings I focused on for my doctoral research. My knowledge was being shared, and in new collaborations, further developed and used.

I had found one of my knowledge ambassadors. She was closer than I thought, and there all along. I'm a little ashamed that I didn't recognize her sooner. However, as an action researcher it is my duty to turn embarrassing moments into learning experiences. Here are some questions to think about that may support you in finding your knowledge ambassador more quickly than I did.

DO YOU HAVE "KNOW-WHO"?

We are related in many ways with the people around us; some are colleagues, some are friends, and some are both. Our personal network contains valuable resources of expertise, emotional support, and enthusiasm that can support us in our daily work and life. Being aware of your own network, and even drawing it out on paper as a constellation of connections, can be illuminating. The more insight you have into your network, the better you are able to identify good knowledge ambassadors. These are often the people closest to you, the ones you trust and feel comfortable with. They are the people who understand and value your work, and are engaged with it.

DO YOU CONSCIOUSLY SHAPE YOUR PERSONAL NETWORK?

It's good to realize that your personal network is not static, but dynamic; people come and go. Colleagues are transferred to other organizations, some are friends for life, some are not. This may seem obvious, but for me this was an important insight, because it means that we can also expand and shape our personal networks for our own purposes, such as sharing the knowledge from our research. I learned from one of the action researchers in my study that you shouldn't wait until your research is completed to build relationships with potential knowledge ambassadors. You should be doing this throughout your research, so that they become invested in your work and your ideas as they evolve. This woman was intentional about involving in her research activities colleagues who could help strengthen the buy-in and future use of her research findings. She explained, "The more people know about your research and think about it with you, the more people you make co-owners of your research, and this will enhance the chance that it will be used in school practice during the next years."

DO YOU REMAIN OPEN AND ALERT TO THE UNEXPECTED OPPORTUNITIES THAT MAY ARISE FROM YOUR PERSONAL NETWORK?

As my story showed, I wasn't so alert and open to grabbing great opportunities, even when they were right in front of me. In my own research, I was struck by the story of an action researcher in the Netherlands who didn't feel much support for her research within her school. However, she didn't get upset. She remained open to opportunities for collaboration and knowledge sharing with colleagues, and ultimately found one in an unexpected context: the smokers' room in the school. In the Netherlands, many schools have such a room (which often resembles a dark dungeon and is the size of a closet) to give teachers an opportunity to smoke indoors. The teacher was a smoker herself, and everyday after school she met with a couple of colleagues from other teams who were also smoking in this room. They shared their experiences, listened to each others' stories, and developed trusting relationships among themselves. She also talked to them about the things she was doing in her research. Her colleagues listened, offered feedback, and eventually, a colleague from another department became enthusiastic. The teacher researcher saw this as an opportunity for collaboration, and invited this colleague to join her action research. Soon they were conducting a collaborative action research study in each other's classrooms. This teacher became the knowledge ambassador for her research findings within the other department. Of course, I'm not urging you to take up smoking, but this story demonstrates that even our bad habits may help connect great people and good ideas.

In our daily practice, many opportunities for collaboration, the exchange of ideas, and knowledge sharing evolve from our interactions with the people in our networks, but do we recognize them? I noticed during my research that often I was the one blocking those opportunities, mainly because they were so unexpected. They didn't fit in my schedule, I didn't know their outcomes, it wasn't the right time or place. To me, that is the challenge: keeping an open mind and being prepared for the unexpected opportunities.

DO YOU LIKE SURPRISES?

It is not easy to predict the outcomes of organic social processes such as building relationships, sharing ideas, and collaborating. There will be surprising outcomes from building your personal networks and finding your knowledge ambassadors. Through the connections of his knowledge ambassador (his research advisor), one of the action researchers in my study found himself teaching in the university program about the method that he had developed in his action research, only 3 months after he completed his study. Another research advisor acted as a knowledge ambassador for her student, and this teacher found herself a couple of weeks later sharing her action research findings together with her pupils' in front of a large audience at a national conference. Since the unexpected connection Marieke made for me at the conference, I've continued the research collaboration with the people from the school in San Diego, expanded my personal network to other researchers at the local university, and 2 years later I'm not living in the Netherlands anymore. Right now, I'm looking at the San Diego sun, writing this chapter as a researcher at that same university, doing research at that same school in San Diego. If there are no more surprises, I might even go to the San Diego Zoo this weekend ...

CHAPTER THIRTY

Confessions OF AN Educational Researcher

Overcoming Cognitive Dissonance about Action Research

NORIYUKI INOUE

FIRST CONTACT

Why do we have to care about research? If someone asks the question now, my response would be, "because it is the coolest thing to do in the world." However, I need to confess that my relationship with research has not been a straightforward one.

Just like many, I was first involved in "research" when I was an undergraduate student. Majoring in engineering science, I felt research was something esoteric (and sometimes unbearably boring) that you are commanded to do by expert scientists. After graduation, I taught mathematics at a high school for 6 years, decided to pursue a graduate degree focused on how students learn and develop, and eventually completed a doctoral program in educational psychology. In the doctoral program, I was fascinated by all the learning opportunities and research apprenticeship experiences available for becoming an educational researcher. There, research meant creating new knowledge and contributing to academic fields by searching for "truths" unknown.

I encountered the idea of action research when I became a tenure-track faculty member at my current institution, where some of my tenured colleagues had decided to incorporate it into our programs. As a faculty member, I would need to start teaching and advising graduate students in action research. However, I found myself struggling to make sense of various aspects of action research, given my background with "research."

CONFESSIONS: COGNITIVE DISSONANCE

The following are my little "confessions" about different forms of cognitive dissonance that I experienced through my encounter with action research, and how I ultimately overcame them.

Is Action Research a Rigorous Kind of Research?

My first take on action research was that it is not a rigorous kind of research. What I heard about action research went against many things I knew about rigorous research. I wondered, if action research is a type of research on context-specific issues, what is the point of such a narrow focus? Wasn't the purpose of research to uncover truths that could be generalized and applied to much wider situations? If action researchers are supposed to personally reflect on experiences, how could the research be free from personal biases? And how is it different from self-serving social advocacy, or romanticized activism in the name of educational research? At that point, it was not clear to me how people doing action research deal with possible biases, and what it meant for action research as a research methodology.

With all these questions in mind, I began reading about action research and engaged in a series of dialogues about these issues with my colleagues and action researchers outside my institution. This was a slow process that required open-mindedness and patience. Through these dialogues, I gradually learned that action research aims at improving real-life practices through action and reflection, rather than uncovering unknown truths. I also learned that action research includes the researcher as the research target, so that the unit of the analysis includes not only those who are taught, but also those who teach and who conduct research (e.g., Torbert, 2004). This inside-out approach made sense to me. I was advising graduate students, some of whom were in-service teachers whose main concern was to improve their practice, but who struggled to do so by merely critically reading and discussing professional and academic articles. According to this inside-out view of educational improvement, traditional research paradigms cannot truly improve educational practice since such research takes place in the outside-in manner, without incorporating those who are inside the practice as well as the personal, professional, and political dimensions of the practice (Noffke, 2009). Rather than disseminating the "truth" found in research labs to practice situations, action research aims at practice improvement by starting from the practitioner and context-specific needs, which could lead to more meaningful and widespread impacts (Inoue, 2015). These realizations clicked in my mind and gradually swept my doubts away. For me, this was a Copernican change in perspective.

At that time, I was involved in a series of research projects on Japanese Lesson Study as a form of educational improvement, and everything we learned in the research pointed in the same direction (see Inoue, 2010, 2011). If the purpose of educational research is to improve educational practice, it should involve educators in transforming our perspectives and our practice. If such "living" moments for self-transformation are absent, it would be hard to truly improve the practice (Whitehead & McNiff, 2006). To me, what seemed biased and trivial at the outset was the aspect of action research aimed at personal transformation, yet through my high school teaching experience and my research on Japanese Lesson Study, I knew this was essential. I realized that the rigor of educational research should reside in its direct connection to self-transformation and professional growth, rather than logically clean and predetermined research procedures alone. Gradually, I began to see that action research had rich potential and catalytic power to improve educational practice.

With this realization, I began to mentor my graduate students' action research projects with more focus on the personal, professional, and context-specific dimensions of their practice for their growth as educators. Through multiple cycles of mentoring my students this way, I found that this new approach substantially promoted practice improvement as well as personal and professional development. At that point, I found myself viewing action research as much more challenging and worthwhile than traditional research. Going through personal and professional development is hard and sometimes messy, but it is what creates more sustainable and real impacts on the quality of teaching (Inoue, 2012). I learned that action research could offer such organic learning experiences often absent in traditional educational research.

Is Action Research Disconnected from Scientific Knowledge about Learning?

As an educational researcher, I had learned that research starts from a comprehensive review of previous research that then points to the need for further research. However, you can start action research from perceived needs related to your practice. To me, this looked like a red flag. I wondered how we could call action research "research" if it is not built on the scientific knowledge base about learning that educational researchers have built over a century. Just look at all the books and articles on educational theories and research in libraries and online databases. Disconnecting ourselves from such a vast knowledge base and going ahead with our own research seemed to be a thoughtless dismissal.

With this doubt in my mind, I emphasized to my students the importance of spending hours in libraries and reading as many articles related to their research topics as possible. I asked my students to justify their actions or interventions in terms of previous studies and to discuss compelling reasons why the research is needed in terms of the existing literature. Needless to say, my students diligently followed my instructions since I was an authority figure for them as their professor.

However, as I advised more and more students' action research projects, I began to realize that the growth and development of my students took place in a substantial manner not because of the legitimacy of their research in terms of the research literature, but because of their reflections on the actions that they actually carried out. I learned that the success of action research was closely tied to the quality of their reflections on their actions and the ways they personally transformed aspects of their practice such as relationship building with their students, developing resilience to accept and learn from failures, understanding others' thinking in their shoes, and patiently exploring new approaches to meet the students' needs in the context. I initially viewed these teacher-/context-specific factors as trivial factors in educational research, but gradually realized that they are quite significant factors that actually predict the quality of practice improvement. I realized that the literature could guide our practice improvement effects, but what truly causes our growth, development, and transformation is our own actions and reflections that we carry out in particular practice situations.

With this new realization, I started incorporating this discussion into my research method classes—discussion about the role and meaningfulness of the existing research for improving educational practice (e.g., "So what?" about the literature). I shared my cognitive dissonance on this issue with my students, and asked them how they could make sense of it. To my surprise, many of my students also wondered about this issue, and we had rich discussions. As I facilitated these discussions, I realized that many of the teachers whom I taught and advised also have had traditional research trainings during their undergraduate years. I was not alone. These discussions included many voices, but they typically ended with consensus that we can gain valuable advice from the literature, but we should be careful in interpreting and applying what the literature suggests by mindfully considering our own specific practice and situation. Most importantly, the literature can give valuable hints for practice improvement as a guide, but should not be regarded as the primary reason to conduct the action research.

Is Action Research Built on Lousy Logic?

When I encountered action research, one of my biggest concerns about the research methodology was how it is possible to reason about the effect of the action without controlling for variables that are outside the scope of the research. In traditional research there are different established ways to control for extraneous variables, but in actual practice situations, it is typically impossible or unethical to enact such controls. I wondered how action research could become free from this internal validity problem—or what I perceived as lousy logic on cause-and-effect relationships.

Perhaps this requires a little more clarification: Action research is a context-specific research, and thus open to so many extraneous variables. Therefore, in action research, there are many real-life and situational factors that will influence the impact of the actions, which makes it difficult to reason about the impact of your actions. For instance, if we were experimenting with the use of certain software for improving our students' learning and found that the students' learning performance improved, how could we tell that the effect was from the use of the software and not from our excitement of doing something new, the students' sense of novelty, or a popular TV program related to the lesson content that most of the students watched last evening? There are so many extraneous factors that could have affected the process and the outcome of the lessons, and I wondered how action researchers could logically reason about the impact of the actions.

As I continued advising action research projects, I noticed that my graduate students juggled these myriad situational and personal factors throughout their action research projects. They engaged in multiple cycles of reflecting on their teaching and obtaining data, many times going beyond the expected scope of their initial research plan. At each point, it was not possible to clearly determine what really caused the improvement, but over time, their action research was evidencing improvement in the forms of students' engagement, learning performance, higher quality of work, and so on. And I saw that the teachers grew as they became more insightful and reflective educators in the action research process.

To me, it was amazing to see such improvement owing to what I initially thought was research built on lousy logic. I realized that action research is a very different kind of research from the one that I had learned in graduate school. Its ultimate goal is not to uncover the universal "truth" from a large data set, or even to uncover the cause and effect between particular variables, but to become a wiser and more mindful practitioner. This does not mean that action researchers should stop logically reasoning about different factors and themes that emerge in the research process. It means that we should embrace the complexity that is revealed through multiple cycles of actions and reflections, and focus our energies and our analysis on practice (see Inoue, 2015). That was a big "Aha!" moment for me. I learned that it is not necessarily strict logical coherency, but being able to deal with logical uncertainty, that serves as the driving force of teacher development and practice improvement.

REFLECTION: DANCING IN MOTION SICKNESS

In attempting to overcome these types of cognitive dissonance, I learned many things about action research as well as the limitations of traditional educational research. These experiences have gradually influenced the ways I viewed educational research as a whole, and in a way, unified my experiences as a teacher and a researcher. I no longer see the complexity of reality as "threats" to research, but as what truly promotes the richness of practice-linked research.

Initially, my experiences with action research created a sense of motion sickness, but that in turn gave me valuable hints to reconceptualize what educational research is all about. In fact, because of these experiences, I now see the sense of motion sickness as an unavoidable feature of any practice improvement effort. For instance, when you drive a car, you are destined to drive over bumpy roads. Similarly, airplanes cannot be totally free from air turbulence as they travel to their destinations. Perhaps this applies to any kind of effort in real-life practice.

I now suspect that it is how you "dance" in the complexity of educational practice that defines who you are as an educational researcher or an educator. Some of us refuse to dance, favoring objective and logical reasoning to nail down "truth." Others dance and dive deeply into the sea of dynamic complexity in spite of motion sickness. I find myself enjoying the latter way of embracing educational research, and am confident that action research offers a rich and promising direction for advancing educational research and practice.

WORKS CITED

Inoue, N. (2010). A cross-cultural approach to deconstructing cognitive processes in the mathematics classroom. In K. D. Keith (Ed.), *Cross-cultural psychology: A contemporary reader* (pp. 198–209). Hoboken, NJ: Wiley/Blackwell.

Inoue, N. (2011). Zen and the art of neriage: Facilitating consensus building in mathematics inquiry lessons through Lesson Study. *Journal of Mathematics Teacher Education, 14*, 5–23.

Inoue, N. (2012). *Mirrors of the mind: An introduction to mindful ways of thinking education.* New York: Peter Lang Publishing.

Inoue, N. (2015). *Beyond actions: Psychology of action research for mindful educational improvement.* New York: Peter Lang Publishing.

Noffke, S. E. (2009). Revisiting the professional, personal, and political dimensions of action research. In S. E. Noffke & B. Somekh (Eds.). *The Sage handbook of educational action research* (pp. 6–25). Los Angeles: Sage.

Torbert, W. R. (2004). *Action inquiry: The secret of timely and transforming leadership.* San Francisco: Berrett-Koehler Publishers.

Whitehead, J., & McNiff, J. (2006). *Action research: Living theory.* Thousand Oaks, CA: Sage.

About THE Contributors

Bernice Alota is a 6th grade teacher at High Tech Middle in Point Loma, California. She received her bachelor's degree in chemistry at the U.S. Naval Academy and her master's in education at the University of San Diego. She also holds three Montessori credentials and was an instructor at the Montessori Center for Teacher Education in San Diego. Bernice conducted her action research in Santee, California. She currently resides in San Diego with her husband, Gervy, and her two children, Baby Gervy and Giselle.

Margit Boyesen teaches a multiage class of 1st, 2nd, and 3rd grade students at Cardiff Elementary in Cardiff-by-the-Sea, California. She's passionate about writing, technology, art, travel, and continuing to grow in the teaching profession. As part of the San Diego Area Writing Project's Leadership Team, she presents professional development to teachers in various districts around San Diego County.

Stacey Caillier, Ph.D. is Director of the Center for Research on Equity and Innovation at the High Tech High Graduate School of Education. She began her career as a high school physics and math teacher and served as principal investigator for a collaborative action research project exploring arts and academic integration in a Northern California charter school. She is currently investigating intersections between teacher identity, teacher leadership, action research, and school culture. She holds degrees from Willamette University and the University of California, Davis.

Frank Cornelissen is a research fellow at the University of California, San Diego and the University of Cambridge (U.K.). Previously, he worked in the field of education as an elementary school teacher, consultant, lecturer, researcher, and senior policy advisor of the Dutch Education Council. His master's thesis on the supervision of teachers' action research has been awarded the national master's thesis award from the Association for Human Resource Development in the Netherlands. In the context of his Ph.D., Frank conducted a case study in one of the High Tech High Schools in San Diego. He explored how teachers who conduct action research develop, share, and use knowledge with their colleagues in school.

Jennifer Edstrom is principal consultant at Edstrom Educational Consulting and a student teaching supervisor at the School of Leadership and Education Sciences at the University of San Diego. She conducted her action research in the form of Japanese Lesson and Learning Study in Cajon Valley School District in San Diego, California, while completing her M.Ed. at the University of San Diego. She has continued this research in conjunction with the University of San Diego and the San Diego Unified School District.

Veronica Garcia is a research associate at the Mobile Technology Learning Center and Center for Education Policy and Law at the University of San Diego. She is also an adjunct professor with the Learning and Teaching Department in the School of Leadership and Education Studies at University of San Diego. The action research project Veronica supported took place in Los Angeles, California. Veronica is co-author of *Critical Media Pedagogies: Teaching for Achievement in City Schools* with Dr. Ernest Morrell, Rudy Duenas, and Jorge Lopez. She has presented at conferences such as the National Council of Teachers of English, the American Educational Research Association, and the Digital Media and Learning Conference.

Samantha Gladwell currently teaches 2nd and 3rd grade at Not Your Ordinary School (NYOS) Charter School in Austin, Texas. Her research on student choice in math learning stations was conducted while teaching 4th grade at San Diego Cooperative Charter School in San Diego, California. Samantha completed her M.Ed. in teacher leadership in the High Tech High Graduate School of Education in 2010. She credits the graduate program with giving her a reflective eye toward her teaching practices and the skills needed to be an effective leader in her classroom and school.

Alyssa Robledo Graham is a 7th grade English teacher at National City Middle School (NCMS) in National City, California. She is in her sixth year of teaching at NCMS and feels fortunate to work in the community where she was raised. Alyssa conducted her action research while student teaching at Sweetwater High School. Mrs. Graham is very active at her site and serves on the school site council, the faculty advisement committee, and as the lead for her English 7 Professional Learning Community (PLC).

Laurel Gustafson is currently in her twenty-seventh year of teaching 2nd grade at Robert Crown Elementary School in Wauconda, Illinois. Recently, she served to help create the new teacher evaluation document used throughout her school district. Laurel felt so strongly about the research she gathered with Cathy Henry that she agreed to share information at a literacy conference and staff development meetings. She continues to incorporate new components into the word study approach to optimize student progress. Her love for teaching is evident, and she believes that research that supports her instruction is re-energizing.

Stephen F. Hamilton is professor of human development at Cornell University and associate director of the Bronfenbrenner Center for Translational Research. As a Fulbright Senior Research Fellow, he spent a year studying Germany's apprenticeship system, then wrote *Apprenticeship for Adulthood: Preparing Youth for the Future*, which helped guide the School-to-Work Opportunities Act of 1994. With Mary Agnes Hamilton he led an action research project exploring four programs that support the transition to adulthood of marginalized youth in Latin America. He taught social studies and English for 3 years in a Washington, D.C., vocational high school. In August 2015 he will become president of the High Tech High Graduate School of Education in San Diego.

Melissa Han is an elementary school teacher in San Diego, California. Her action research was conducted while obtaining her Master's of Education in Teacher Leadership at High Tech High Graduate School of Education. Melissa is currently a doctoral candidate at UCSD/CSUSM Educational Leadership Joint Doctorate program and a recipient of the Janet Hageman Chrispeels Doctoral Fellowship in Educational Leadership.

Catherine Henry holds a master's degree in teaching special education from National Louis University in Wheeling, Illinois. The research for this project was conducted in a 2nd grade classroom at Robert Crown Elementary School in Wauconda, Illinois, where Catherine works as a learning behavior specialist. It brings her great pride to know that this research was an instrument for change and created fair and meaningful learning opportunities for all students.

Janet Ilko currently teaches English language development and leadership courses at Cajon Valley Middle School in El Cajon, California. She is passionate about inspiring student voice and choice, and uses writing and technology as a means to inspire students to share their stories and opinions, with a focus on social justice and equity. She is a fellow with the San Diego Area Writing Project, and has written several articles for *The Dialogue* and *NWP Digital Is*. She documents her work with students and the students' own work on two sites, http://www.writinginmyhand.org and http://www.writingforchange.net.

Noriyuki Inoue, Ph.D., is an associate professor at the University of San Diego, School of Leadership and Education Sciences. He specializes in the areas of educational psychology, educational research methods, teacher expertise development, action research, Japanese Lesson Study, and mathematics education. He is now actively involved in advancing scholarship in the areas of action research and teacher development, and is known for cross-cultural research incorporating East Asian cultural concepts and epistemology for professional development. He received an M.Ed. from Harvard University and an M.A. and Ph.D. from Columbia University.

Makeba Jones is an assistant teaching professor in the Department of Education Studies at University of California, San Diego. She teaches courses on the social organization of education and on language, culture, and education. She also teaches a course that prepares undergraduates to serve as tutors and mentors in local schools, and a course on action research for undergraduates. Her research interests include urban education, school reform, youth engagement, and inequality in schooling. Makeba has published numerous articles, reports, and book chapters about her work.

Qudsia Kalsoom is working as an assistant professor and chair in the Department of Professional Studies at Ali Institute of Education in Lahore, Pakistan. She conducted her action research in Beaconhouse School System, a private school chain in Pakistan. Qudsia has been involved in mentoring preservice and in-service teachers, conducting research, supervising research, and teaching courses on curriculum studies, pedagogy, and research methods. She is on the editorial committee of *AIE Journal for Research and Innovation in Education,* published by Ali Institute of Education.

Jessica De Young Kander is a full-time lecturer at Eastern Michigan University, where she teaches children's literature courses. She holds a B.A. in education from the University of Michigan and M.A.s in children's literature and the teaching of writing from Eastern Michigan University.

Heather Lattimer is an associate professor and chair of the Department of Learning and Teaching in the School of Leadership and Education Sciences at the University of San Diego (USD). Her areas of research focus on teacher education and professional development, secondary education, adolescent literacy, and international education. A former middle and high school teacher, Heather is the author of several professional texts for teachers, including *Thinking through Genre* (Stenhouse, 2003) and *Real World Literacies* (NCTE, 2014). She holds degrees from Harvard, Stanford, and the University of California, San Diego.

Laura McNaughton is an assistant director of residential education at Occidental College, located in Northeast Los Angeles. Before coming to Occidental, Laura was a graduate student at the University of San Diego and studied higher education leadership. While at USD, Laura also worked as a graduate assistant in the Student Leadership and Involvement Center. Through this position and her studies in the School of Leadership, Laura took a group of students to Peru, where she conducted her action research focusing on engaging students in social justice through international immersion experiences.

Bryan Meyer worked for the High Tech High Schools from 2010 to 2014, and is currently a mathematics coach for the Escondido Union High School District. His action research through the High Tech High Graduate School of Education focused on the intersections of epistemology, identity, agency, and mathematical habits of mind. His work in the field is centered around creating space for teachers to collaborate with one another, to reinvent their practice together, and to enact change against the societal inequities that mathematics education is reproducing.

Rob Meza-Ehlert is a vice principal at the School of Digital Media & Design at the Kearny High Educational Complex in San Diego, California. Through years as a high school social studies teacher and adjunct professor of education at the University of San Diego, Rob learned the power of collaborative approaches to teaching and learning. When the school day is done, Rob likes nothing better than to spend time with his wife, children, and good friends.

Melissa King Moxley is a K–8 non-public school administrator specializing in students with special needs. Her current assignment is in the San Fernando Valley of Southern California.

Jocelyn Peck is a 9th grade math and physics teacher at High Tech High International in San Diego, California. She conducted her action research while teaching math at a neighboring school, High Tech High Media Arts. She is passionate about building student engagement in the STEM fields, both in and outside the classroom. She has started an astronomy club at her school that takes students on monthly camping trips out of the city to see the stars. She is also an amateur telescope maker and the reigning limbo champion among the school faculty.

Linnea L. Rademaker is a graduate school dissertation chair at Northcentral University. The chapters in this volume describe work Linnea engaged in collaboratively with Cathy Henry and Laurel Gustafson in their elementary school setting. Linnea serves in leadership positions in the Action Research Network of the Americas (ARNA, http://www.arnaconnect.org) and the Action Research SIG of the American Educational Research Association. Prior to her current position Linnea taught action research courses to preservice and in-service teachers at National Louis University in Chicago.

Juli Ruff has been teaching for over 16 years in a range of settings. She has taught adjudicated youth while canoeing the swamps of Florida, public middle schoolers in Idaho, and gifted artists at a private art school. She currently teaches 9th grade at High Tech High, a project-based charter school in San Diego. She completed her action research at the HTH Graduate School of Education and published her work in a book, *Peer Collaboration and Critique: Using Student Voices to Improve Student Work.*

Daisy Sharrock teaches 10th grade math and chemistry at High Tech High in San Diego, California, and is also an adjunct professor for the High Tech High Graduate School of Education. She is currently enrolled in the educational leadership doctorate program at the University of California, San Diego, where her research interests include student motivation and the development of reflective education practitioners and their impact on school culture. Her masters work on grit, motivation, and scientific inquiry was completed though the High Tech High Graduate School of Education in conjunction with the Reuben H. Fleet Science Center in San Diego.

JoHanna Simko is an administrator at High Tech High Chula Vista, where she works as a project-based learning coach. Her action research was conducted at HTHCV while teaching 12th grade English. Additionally, JoHanna is a professional learning specialist at the University of San Diego with the Mobile Technology Learning Center, where she supports effective teaching and learning initiatives at various district within San Diego.

Tony Spitzberg performed his action research at High Tech Middle Media Arts in a 6th grade humanities class. He is currently teaching middle school at Innovations Academy Charter School in San Diego. Tony was recently recognized by the Scholastic Art and Writing Awards as an Outstanding Educator whose dedication, commitment, and guidance are represented by student work selected for national honors. He also won NETGEAR's national WiFi My School writing contest in 2013, which awarded his school a state-of-the-art network upgrade.

Callie Sprague is a 7th grade humanities teacher at High Tech Middle Chula Vista in San Diego. She conducted her action research at Paul Ecke Central Elementary School in Encinitas, California. Callie earned her bachelor's degree from Providence College and her master's degree in education from the University of San Diego.

Cady Staff has been working with High Tech High schools for the past 10 years, and currently teaches 8th grade humanities at High Tech Middle Chula Vista. She taught high school English at San Diego High School and Madison High School before she began teaching at High Tech Middle Media Arts in 2005, the year it opened. In 2012 she spent a year abroad working with Innovation Unit and schools in England transitioning to project-based learning.

Sarah Strong is in her ninth year working for the High Tech High organization, and this year is teaching 10th grade math part-time, and supporting new math teachers the rest of the time. She also has been working with other local schools doing consulting with their math program as they transition to common core. She conducted her action research when she was teaching 6th grade math/science in 2008 at High Tech Middle, and her findings continue to inform her practice today.

Ashley Vasquez teaches 5th grade at Finney Elementary School in Chula Vista, California. She grew up in Kailua-Kona, Hawaii, and later received a B.A. in liberal studies with a minor in Spanish from the University of San Diego. She received her master's degree in education from the Teacher Leadership Program at High Tech High Graduate School of Education. She is the author of *Community Service Learning in the Elementary Classroom* and "Sharing Bright Spots, Ending Isolation," published in the spring 2012 edition of High Tech High's *UnBoxed*. She is currently pursuing an administrative credential at the University of San Diego.

Stacey Williams teaches a global gap year program, leading groups of students around the world to study international development, community engagement, and social justice between high school and university. Her chapter centers on research conducted at the University of San Diego's (USD) Women's Center, where she served as the graduate assistant coordinating leadership development programs. She went on to write about her action research in a thesis, *Belonging, Believing, and Being: A Journey Toward Social Justice at the University of San Diego's Women's Center*, which earned her Action Research Project of the Year at USD's master's in higher education leadership program. With all of this, Stacey is passionate about working with college students as they ask questions of themselves and of the world.

Critical Pedagogical Perspectives

Greg S. Goodman, *General Editor*

Educational Psychology: Critical Pedagogical Perspectives is a series of relevant and dynamic works by scholars and practitioners of critical pedagogy, critical constructivism, and educational psychology. Reflecting a multitude of social, political, and intellectual developments prompted by the mentor Paulo Freire, books in the series enliven the educator's process with theory and practice that promote personal agency, social justice, and academic achievement. Often countering the dominant discourse with provocative and yet practical alternatives, *Educational Psychology: Critical Pedagogical Perspectives* speaks to educators on the forefront of social change and those who champion social justice.

For further information about the series and submitting manuscripts, please contact:

Dr. Greg S. Goodman
Department of Education
Clarion University
Clarion, Pennsylvania
ggoodman@clarion.edu

To order other books in this series, please contact our Customer Service Department at:

(800) 770-LANG (within the U.S.)
(212) 647-7706 (outside the U.S.)
(212) 647-7707 FAX

Or browse online by series at:

www.peterlang.com